WISDOM

FOR THE

WORLD

AND

MINDFUL ADVICE
TO MY NATION

The REQUISITES *of* RECONCILIATION

Venerable Sayadaw U Pandita of Burma
in Conversation with Alan Clements

..

BY ALAN CLEMENTS
ASSISTED BY FERGUS HARLOW

WORLD DHARMA PUBLICATIONS

©2019

WISDOM
FOR THE
WORLD
AND
MINDFUL ADVICE
TO MY NATION

The **REQUISITES** *of* **RECONCILIATION**

Venerable Sayadaw U Pandita of Burma
in Conversation with Alan Clements

..

BY ALAN CLEMENTS
ASSISTED BY FERGUS HARLOW

WORLD DHARMA PUBLICATIONS

WWW.WORLDDHARMA.COM

WWW.WISDOMFORTHEWORLD.COM

Published in 2019 by World Dharma Publications

Cover design by World Dharma Publications
Typography by World Dharma Publications

Library of Congress Cataloging-in-Publication Data
Clements, Alan 1951 —

Wisdom for the World
Mindful Advice to My Nation
The Requisites of Reconciliation
Venerable Sayadaw U Pandita of Burma
In Conversation with Alan Clements

p. cm.
ISBN-13: 978-0-9894883-1-0
Biography 2. International Relations. 3. Political. 4. Liberty — freedom — Buddhism
5. Spiritual life — Buddhism — non-sectarian 6. Human rights — all aspects 7. Social,
Political and Environmental justice — all 8. Activism — all 9. Consciousness — all
        10. Politics — global 11. Body, Mind & Spirit

First Printing, February 2019
ISBN-13: 978-0-9894883-1-0
Printed in the USA on acid-free, recycled paper

World Dharma Publications
www.WorldDharma.com
www.WisdomfortheWorld.com

Dedicated to national reconciliation in Burma,
the end of discrimination, violence, and war,
the release of all prisoners of conscience,
the thriving of a peaceful democracy
with regard for rule of law
and global human rights.
PEACE

Venerable Sayadaw U Pandita

In Conversation with Alan Clements
Panditarama Meditation Center,
Yangon, Myanmar

••

WISDOM FOR THE WORLD
AND
MINDFUL ADVICE TO MY NATION

INTRODUCTION

..

For the last thirty-seven years of his life, Sayadaw U Pandita was my spiritual teacher, my life mentor, and my friend. In the early years of that period, I was a monk living at the Mahasi Thathana Yeiktha, the monastery in Yangon which had been founded by Mahasi Sayadaw in 1947 and which had been Sayadaw U Pandita's home since 1954. He later moved to his own monastery, Panditarama, where I visited him in the months before he died. It was here that I was privileged to have nine nights of profound conversations with him. These were among his final teachings. He died forty-five days later on April 16, 2016 at the age of ninety-five. This book is the edited record of those conversations, his offering on the way of reconciliation for a troubled world.

By the time of his passing, he had been in the monastic order within Burma for eighty-three years, having ordained as a novice monk as an orphan at the age of twelve. During his years at Mahasi Thathana Yeiktha he became a senior meditation teacher and founded an annual four-week Buddhist Culture course specifically for children in the development of "mindful intelligence." When Mahasi Sayadaw passed away in 1982 Sayadaw U Pandita was appointed the Ovadcariya Sayadaw (Head Monk) of the monastery. As the senior teacher, he was for many years the spiritual advisor to Aung San Suu Kyi and other leaders in Burma's democracy movement and had been influential in honing their strategies of nonviolence. Over the years, he also became the *dhamma* teacher to many thousands of Asian and Western students worldwide.

I met Sayadaw U Pandita within a few months of my arrival at Mahasi Thathana Yeiktha in 1979. He was already a senior teacher at that time, and on our first meeting we talked well into the night. Despite not having traveled much at that point, he had a vast knowledge of science, literature, culture, art, and, of course, classical Buddhist teachings and in particular, *vipassanā* (mindfulness practice). He spoke several languages and could quote at will from, say, Tolstoy to an obscure Buddhist text from the 1920s. Often in the middle of a discussion he would cheerfully pull a passage from one of the thousands of books in his greeting room at the monastery. A great conversationalist, he also had a natural curiosity about his young western guest and wanted to know all about my life growing up in America: what were my interests as a child, my difficulties, my education. Thus began a cross-cultural understanding that was to deepen over the decades. Perhaps we educated each other in the differences of how eastern and western minds are conditioned.

I was dazzled by his brilliance and his kindness to me, and I think he found in me a novice in need of direction. I asked for and was granted permission for him to be my primary teacher there in that exotic land of Burma in which I found myself, eager to come to terms with my mind, living as a monk in a monastery far from home.

Eventually, I made my way back to my own homeland but Sayadaw U Pandita and I never lost touch. I organized his first trips to America and Australia and I went regularly back to Burma to visit him and to continue our exploration of the deeper streams of life. His wisdom and intellect only grew with time.

Although these nine nights of conversation cover a wide range of subjects, in the end Sayadaw U Pandita's passion was to convey the importance of finding ways to live in harmony with each other. He could see the trends in the world and their potential for political and social strife. As someone who had lived through World War II along with the more recent troubles in Burma, he also knew the limits of force, hatred, and abuse of power. His lifelong message was that peace is only possible through communication and understanding. Thus, he spent some of his last moments on earth emphasizing these ideals in the art of dialogue, which was his particular genius.

Alan Clements
SEPTEMBER 18, 2018

BIOGRAPHY

..

Ashin Paṇḍitābhivaṃsa, the Panditarama Shwe Taung Gon
Meditation Center Sayadawgyi, was born on Thursday,
July 28, 1921 in the Shwebo Su quarter of Tadah Kalei Village
in Yangon. His parents were U Hpe and Daw Chit Su. He was
the ninth of ten children. When he was four years old, his mother
passed away. When he was ten, his father passed away.

At age seven he began his dhamma education under the
tutelage of Sayadaw U Jāgara in the village monastery of Kaw
Che, Bago Division. As a schoolboy he passed the Pahtama Ngay
and Pahtama Lat oral examinations in Buddhist scripture held
by the Dakkhinayone Shwe Kyin Daik in Kawa Township. At
age twelve, he ordained as a novice monk under the supervision
of Sayadaw U Jāgara.

At age eighteen, he went to study under the great Sayadaw
Ashin Kelasa of the Mahabodhi Forest Monastery in the village
of Kyauk in Bago Township. There he passed the Kyauk Tan

Mahabodhi Forest Monastery Oral Scriptural examinations for the Pahtama Kyi level.

When he reached twenty years of age, on the eighth waning day of Dapou Dweh in 1302 (1941), he became a fully ordained monk with the sponsorship of U Bo Han and Daw Thaung of Kyauk Tan in the Khanda Sima hall of the Mahabodhi Forest Monastery. His preceptor was Mahabodhi Sayadaw U Kelasa.

During World War II, he was an assistant teacher at the Kyaikkasan New Shwe Kyin Daik Study Center in Thinghan Kyun Township. During that period, in 1308 at the age of 26, he passed the examinations for Pahtama Lat in the first ever Pali Pahtama Pyan Examinations.[1] He passed the Pahtama Kyi examinations in 1309 as well as the Cetiyangana Pariyatti examinations[2] for students.

In 1311 at the age of 28 he went to Mandalay to study at the new Mahavisuddhayone Study Center under the guidance of Zi Pin Sayadaw Ashin Sujatatthera. He studied the Pali, Commentaries and Subcommentaries related to the Dhammacariya level of study under many excellent teachers. He also studied in Yangon under Saya-gyi U Aung Myat at the Phaya Kyi Daik and with Ashin Vasetthabhivamsa of the Than Lyin Thapyaykan Dhammikarama Study Center. In 1313, at the age of 30, he passed the Siripavara Dhammacariya and Sasanadhaja Siripavara Dhammacariya exams. The following year, he passed the Cetiyangana Teaching Level Examination, taking first place.

---

1 These are Pali examinations sponsored by the government. Pali examinations were held in the days of the kings, under the British and are also held today. Nowadays there are exams sponsored by the government as well as exams sponsored by associations. The exams can be oral or written. The government degree is the standard qualification.
2 The Cetiyangana examinations are sponsored by an organization.

While living at Kyaikkasan Shwe Kyin Monastery, he studied English with Saya-gyi U Hpe Thin. They made an agreement that whoever saw the Dhamma first would tell the other. Saya-gyi went to Mahasi Sasana Yeiktha in Yangon, practiced, and became satisfied and inspired. He then went to the Shwe-Taung Gon Sayadaw-to-be and urged him to practice under the guidance of Mahasi Sayadaw. Therefore, in 1312, at the age of 29, he approached Mahasi Sayadaw and receiving his instructions, began the practice of Satipaṭṭhāna under the tutelage of Ashin Vicāra. He became firmly convinced that only when Pariyatti is followed by practical experience would he gain a firm footing in the teachings of the Buddha. After he practiced, the intention arose in him to spread the Dhamma to the whole world, beginning with his close relatives and companions.

He had the desire for others to know and experience the taste of the Dhamma, which is many times better than all the other tastes of the world, and for others to beautify their lives and develop their virtues with the Dhamma. In 1316, at age 33, while he was teaching Pali, he participated in the Sixth Great Sangha Council as both Reciter and Corrector of Pali.

In the following year, he went to Mahasi Sayadaw to continue his work of Vipassana and carried out the responsibility given to him by Mahasi Sayadaw.

In 1320, at the age of 37, he accompanied Mahasi Sayadaw to Colombo, Sri Lanka, for the opening of a new meditation center. He taught the Dhamma there in accordance with the instructions of Mahasi Sayadaw for nearly three years before returning to Myanmar due to poor health. In Myanmar he studied profound scripture and practice under the direct guidance of Mahasi Sayadaw, and during that time also instructed yogis who came to practice according to the Mahasi method.

In 1340, or 1979, at the age of 57 he was appointed Nayaka Sayadaw and in 1982, after the passing away of the most Venerable Mahasi Sayadaw, he was appointed sole Ovadacariya of Mahasi Sasana Yeiktha, a post he held for eight years. In 1990, at the age of 68, he founded Panditarama Shwe Taung Gon Sasana Yeiktha in Yangon. With a broad vision that included the Sasana of the future, he worked tirelessly to preach the Dhamma of the Buddha in accordance with the instructions of Mahasi Sayadaw, encompassing both scripture and practice so that neither is omitted.

There are many yogis, both foreign and local, who have had the chance to take shelter under the shade of Panditarama Sayadawgyi's Silā, Samādhi and Paññā, and to absorb the nourishment of the Dhamma, having come to see its virtues through Sayadawgyi's great Mettā and keen determination.

Following heart surgery in 2007 at age 86, the momentum of Sayadawgyi's teaching increased in a manner inconsistent with his age. In addition to holding an annual 60-day special retreat at the Panditarama Hse Main Gone Forest Center, he travelled on Dhamma missions to the United States, Taiwan, Nepal and Singapore.

Within Myanmar, Centers are now located in Yangon, Bago, Than Lyin, Mawlamyaing, Kywe Khyan, Pyin Oo Lwin, Htauk Kyant and Hle Gu. Overseas centers are located in Nepal, Australia, Korea, England, USA, Canada, Malaysia, Singapore and Taiwan. These spread the light of the Dhamma far and wide.

All the centers work hand in hand to spread the Sasana of Practice which includes Scripture and the Sasana of Scripture which includes Practice, in accordance with the high-level desire of their benefactor, the Panditarama Shwe Taung on

Sayadawgyi. Starting from 2010, an annual Dhamma Family Gathering has been held so that all the centers, both within Myanmar and abroad, can listen to Sayadaw-gyi's guidance together in order to carry out their projects uniformly and so that Sāsanā work can continue long into the future. 2016 marked the 7th annual Gathering.

While putting all his energy into promoting the Sāsanā, Practice intertwined with Scripture and Scripture intertwined with Practice, Sayadawgyi passed away on Saturday, the 9th waxing day of Dagu, 1377 (16 April 2016) at 7:35 a.m. at the age of 95 years, 75 vassas.

"REQUISITES *for* RECONCILIATION"

..

ALAN CLEMENTS: Allow me to start by saying how grateful I am for the opportunity to speak with you. My intention in speaking with you is rooted in *dhamma*, seeking your wisdom in illuminating the way beyond fear, anger, and delusion. I have known you for thirty-seven years and have known you to only speak what is true and beneficial. It is for that reason that I seek your advice and insights into what is most beneficial for the people of your country as well as everyone in the world.

My first question: For anyone who has been violated, it is common to react with hurt, anger, even outrage, and at times, seek revenge. As we know, many millions of people in your country have been oppressed for over fifty years by a succession of dictatorships. What advice can you offer the oppressed, especially those harboring feelings of hostility and retribution? How to overcome those feelings of anger and revenge and restrain from acting on them?

VENERABLE SAYADAW U PANDITA: Forbearance is the best. It is what the Buddha taught. Social problems are sure to happen in human society. There are things one likes and things one doesn't like. One smiles at what one likes and scowls at what one doesn't like. It is important to have forbearance – the ability to withstand these swings. Forbearance should be developed from the start, before problems occur. One should make it strong.

In this country we say, "*Khanti* is the highest austerity." In the human world, we are certain to encounter things we do not like. If every time one encounters such things, there is no forbearance and one retaliates, there will be no end to human problems. There will only be quarrels.

To be patient and forbear fully, there must be the ability to logically reason. Without forbearance, a fight occurs, both sides get hurt and there's no relief. And many wrongs are done. When one can forbear, the quarrel quiets. This is the benefit gained.

In this, one needs to add *mettā* – the desire for another's welfare. When the desire for the welfare of others becomes strong, one can be patient and forbearing. When harmed one can forgive, one can give up one's own benefit and make sacrifices. Problems occur because people are not able to have this attitude of *mettā* - the desire for another's welfare.

AC: To end the cycle of conflict, first neutralize one's reaction?

SUP: There are two kinds of enemies or danger: the danger of *akusala* and the danger in the form of a person. *Akusala* are the unwholesome deeds which occur when *lobha* (desire, selfishness), *dosa* (anger, cruelty, hatred) and *moha* (delusion, stupidity) are extreme. These are called the internal enemy. They are also called the nearest danger. Danger in the form of a person is also an enemy: someone who is hostile to us. The Buddha practiced to gradually weaken the internal enemies until they disappeared.

If one cares for oneself and can reason, "When the danger of *akusala*, unwholesome deeds based on *lobha*, *dosa*, and *moha* occurs, there's no end to human problems – there's no relief, neither for myself nor for others. Therefore, one should control oneself." If one restrains oneself and comes to understand the benefit of doing so, when one's forbearance becomes strong, problems are naturally resolved. Since it's important to resolve social problems, the main quality needed to do this is forbearance. And in order to have forbearance, one must have *mettā* as well as compassion.

AC: What is the basis, the spiritual or moral motivation, to restrain *akusala*?

SUP: One should be disgusted by *akusala* as if it were excrement. And one should shrink from doing *akusala* just as one would shrink from picking up a red-hot coal. With a healthy disgust and fear, understanding that *akusala* gives us trouble, one can refrain from wrong-doing.

Further, there should be consideration for others. One should spare others because one understands how they would feel if harmed. That is important. *Hirī* and *ottappa* [moral shame and moral fear] and consideration for others are the qualities which motivate one to refrain from doing *akusala* – unwholesome deeds.

If *lobha* (greed) and *dosa* (anger) arise in us, one will easily break one's *sīla* (moral integrity). One should be disgusted by breaking *sīla*, just as one would be disgusted by excrement. One should be disgusted by the lack of shame and the lack of fear, just as if these were feces. Being without shame and fear, one becomes brash. One should fear being without moral shame and moral fear as one would fear touching a red-hot coal. When one possesses moral shame and moral fear, who would pick up excrement? Who would pick up a red-hot coal? It would burn one. These are the first mental attitudes to arise.

To explain this in material terms, if one wears white clothing in the hot sun, it won't absorb heat. It will reflect the rays of the sun. If one wears black clothing, it will be hot. Lack of moral shame and fear is like wearing black in the sun. These qualities absorb base actions, speech, and mental attitudes. *Hirī* and *ottappa*, like the color white, repel unwholesomeness. People need to know this.

They are also called the *Deva Dhammas*. *Deva dhamma* means dhammas (practices or trainings) which make virtues brilliant. When one lacks these, one's human virtues fade. The quality of behaving like a human being, being able to keep one's mentality humane, having human intelligence, being able to develop special human knowledge – all these human virtues fade without *hirī* and *ottappa*. When one has these qualities, one's virtues become bright. They are the dhammas that make human virtues shine.

They are also called the *loka pāla* dhammas. *Loka pāla* means the 'Guardians of the World.' They preserve the world, keep it from being destroyed. What's important here is one's own individual world as well as the world around one. These qualities preserve one's own individual world so that it is not destroyed. The stronger they are, the more secure one's own world is, and equally, one no longer harms the world around one. The world around one is peaceful.

AC: Allow me to ask: here in Myanmar, the newly elected leaders along with the vast majority of citizens, have stated their desire for "National Reconciliation" - societal harmony based on a policy of loving-kindness, non-hostility, and non-retribution. You have advised how the oppressed can do their part to both heal themselves and society. What role can the oppressors play in healing the nation – moving forward towards a safer, more peaceful and prosperous future, with respect for rule of law, democratic principles, and universal human rights?

SUP: Only if there is no selfish desire for oneself or for one's own group will there be the attitude of wanting good things for the people of this country.

Wanting to have the best only for oneself or for one's group is *lobha*, or greed – extreme greed. If extreme greed is forceful, then *mettā-karuṇā*, or loving kindness and compassion, will dry up. Only if there is *mettā* and *karuṇā* will one be happy to see another's welfare. One will want others to be well, just like oneself. One should also develop *muditā*, or joy at seeing another's good situation. If there is no *mettā* and *karuṇā*, there will be no *muditā*. There will only be envy and miserliness.

Those who have done wrong should correct it by *dhamma* means, just like when a monk commits a monastic offense. They should make an honest admission: 'This act and that act were wrong. I ask your forgiveness.' No matter how great the fault, about half [the people] would be satisfied with this. They will have *mettā* (loving-kindness) [for those who confess their wrong].

A hero, a person who is courageous, has the courage to admit one's mistakes, one's faults. Such a person also has the courage to do things that are beneficial for society. The most effective way to create peace among the people is for the oppressors to courageously admit their faults and reconcile with the oppressed. That is the best.

AC: Is there any further advice you might offer the oppressors to begin this essential process of national reconciliation and peace-building?

SUP: One should understand: wrongs done because of selfish greed and devoid of *mettā* and *karuṇā*, bring only bad results. On the other hand, tasks done without selfishness, and with *mettā* and *karuṇā* present, bring only good results. One should understand the nature of good and bad results. Due to extreme *lobha* and *dosa*, neither knowing the bad results of lacking *mettā* and *karuṇā* nor the good results with *mettā* and *karuṇā* at the forefront, there is blind stupidity. There is darkness. And with darkness, one can't see. As long as this understanding is absent, one lacks moral shame and moral fear.

AC: And the cycle of oppression continues?

SUP: Without *hirī* and *ottappa*, there is *akusala* (unwholesome actions). With *hirī* and *ottappa* (moral shame and moral fear) there is pure clean *kusala* (wholesome actions). That is important.

What should one do to prevent problems from occurring in the world? There should be both control and preservation, so that one's personal world is not destroyed and the world outside one is protected from harm. And if there were a great number of people who kept their own individual world from being destroyed (by restraining unwholesome thoughts, speech and actions), the world would become peaceful.

Another way to foster self-restraint is to have consideration for others. When thoughts, speech and actions are strong enough to cause suffering, reflect: just as I do not wish to suffer, neither do others wish to suffer. As such, one avoids doing harm. Being able to put oneself in another's place is very important.

AC: What is the word for this?

SUP: Empathy: reflecting on yourself and knowing that just as you like happiness, so too others like happiness. This is important for human beings. Having moral shame and moral fear, if one avoids doing wrong due to not wanting to defile oneself, not only are one's actions and speech clean, but others are not harmed. Alternatively, out of consideration, one protects others so as not to harm them or make them suffer mentally or physically. By protecting others, one keeps oneself from doing wrong. This two-fold protection is essential.

AC: Your country has been ruled for decades by corrupt leaders, and those leaders had support, "cronies", as you call them here in Myanmar, friends, family members, colleagues, business acquaintances, subordinates – who were corrupted, and in turn, corrupted others. And through this collusion, the country functioned as a cycle of corruption. The entire apparatus of dictatorship, as I understand it, was a lucrative business based upon a culture of corruption. What single piece of dhamma advice can you offer to transform Myanmar's corruption?

SUP: When an infant lacked breast milk and has already grown up malnourished, scrawny and stunted, with poor physical stamina, one can no longer give breast milk. One can't give baby food to correct this any more. It is only important to develop a new generation. One has to simply focus on that.

AC: Is there a cure for the older generation?

SUP: For them, the best way is to practice the *dhamma*. This is my experience. There were some officers who came to practice after they were fired [during the U Ne Win period]. When they came to see the nature of the *dhamma* due to their practice, they came to know that *dhamma* is the most important thing. They gained firm ground on which to stand. It wasn't possible to teach them starting from the basics. Therefore, the best thing for them was to come and practice. For those people, that is the best method for becoming a good person.

AC: The meditation cure?

SUP: Firstly, one must gain victory over oneself. One has to gain victory over one's own bad habits. More important than victory over external enemies is to first gain internal victory. The Buddha taught how to overcome the internal enemy.

Starting from the age a child can speak, just as one nurses an infant and feeds him or her baby food, parents who know their duties should teach their children well. That is the most basic plan. The children taught according to this plan become cultured and obedient. If they marry a person with the same up-bringing, the child they bear will have a good early start. After the child is born, the parents teach the child good habits. Later, before marriage, when the child practices meditation, he or she gains practical experience. Overall, one needs to have a plan to provide children with the initial seed of Buddhism, to develop good habits and gain practical experience of the *dhamma*.

Because people try to conquer others instead of gaining victory over themselves, there are problems. The Buddha taught that one should simply gain victory over oneself. He taught the method for gaining complete self-victory. If one conquers oneself, the good *devas* (celestial beings) won't sit still. They will protect that person. If one doesn't master oneself but gives up and commits immoral deeds, the *devas* will never come and help.

If one has been born a human being, there are rules. Like driving a car, one should understand the rules of the road. In America, they drive on the right. One should drive the proper speed and be careful. If the light is green, go forward. If it's red, stop. Life can be likened to driving a car. If one follows the rules then one doesn't suffer due to mistakes, and one doesn't hurt others either. But one can still suffer when others are in the wrong. So, one must be careful about this too.

Human beings have rules and duties. If one follows the rules and fulfills one's responsibilities, then one is not at fault. The five precepts (1. not killing. 2. not stealing. 3. refraining from sexual misconduct. 4. refraining from telling lies 5. refraining from the use of intoxicating substances) are the basic rules of for human beings. And to help others when it is beneficial and suitable is a human duty. The five precepts are not only to be kept by Buddhists. All human beings, if they want to be truly human, should keep them. Not knowing this is to be blind and stupid. One's beliefs go the wrong way and one commits acts of violence.

AC: Speaking of *devas*, with the human world fraught with extreme struggles, from famines to world wars and far too many genocides, dangers everywhere, inside and outside, why not dedicate one's everyday *dhamma* practice to becoming a *deva* and carrying on in a higher plane of existence, where, I assume, it's far easier to attain higher stages of awakening?

SUP: Much more important than wishing to become a *deva* is to practice the dhamma to completion while in the human world. If one goes to a *deva* world without having developed the dhamma to completion, when one gets there one forgets about *kusala* (wholesome deeds).

Better than the *deva* realms or the human realms, is to just have one lifetime. When the Buddha-to-be was born in the *deva* realms with a very long life span, he wasn't able to fulfill *pāramī* (the work of someone who is an excellent person). He performed *adhimutti-kāla-kiriyā*, or a sort of *deva*-suicide. Before the end of his life-span, he let go of that existence, because in it he had no opportunity to fulfill the *pāramīs*.

The human world is the best for fulfilling pāramī (the ten perfections: 1. *Dāna pāramī*: generosity; 2. *Sīla pāramī*: virtue, morality; 3. *Nikkhama pāramī*: renunciation; 4. *Paññā pāramī*: liberating wisdom, insight; 5. *Viriya pāramī*: energy, effort; 6. *Khanti pāramī*: patient forbearance; 7. *Sacca pāramī*: truthfulness, honesty; 8. *Adhiṭṭhāna pāramī*: determination, resolution; 9. *Mettā pāramī*: loving-kindness; 10. *Upekkhā pāramī*: equanimity). The human world is a place where if you can live free of fault, you go up. If you are a stupid fool, you go down. That is the human world.

AC: May I ask what evidence you have of rebirth?

SUP: I am a disciple of the Buddha, therefore I follow the path of the Buddha. According to the *Paticca Sammuppāda* [the teaching of Dependent Origination,] cause and effect continue.

AC: What is the motivation to become a Buddha?

SUP: Look at the *Bodhisattva's* motivation to become the *Buddha Gotama*. When he met *Buddha Dipankara*, he had the potential to cut off any further lifetimes. But he also wanted to help beings who were not yet free of the dangers of old age, sickness and death. Without help, they would suffer. With that vision and compassion, he relinquished the opportunity he had at hand to realize the fruition knowledge of an *arahant* (a fully enlightened being). As such, he had to endure suffering. One must say that the basis for this was reasoning power and compassion.

The *Bodhisattva's* reasoning power showed him the way to start fulfilling the *pāramīs* in order to become a Buddha. He reflected that if one doesn't know the true dhamma oneself, it won't be possible to teach it to others. In order to master the true dhamma one needs to fulfill the *paramīs* beginning with *dāna* (generosity). After fulfilling the *paramīs*, the Buddha practiced *satipaṭṭhāna* (the four foundations of mindfulness) and put an end to the kilesas (unwholesome states of mind). When the kilesas were dried up, delusion (*moha*) or ignorance (*avijjā*) was included. Because *avijjā* was eliminated, when the Buddha reflected, he could know whatever was to be known. For the Buddha to assist others, he knew that it was essential to first be complete with self-knowledge. If one wants to give food and clothing to those who are poor, it is only possible when one has something to give. One has to work to gain that something.

Further, only if one has compassion will one want to help. There are four kinds of people: The person who knows for him or herself but is unable to give that knowledge to others. The one who doesn't know for himself but tries to teach others. The one who first practices himself and teaches that to others. The one who neither practices nor gives the practice to others. The Buddha was the type of person who first practiced and then gave the method of practice to others. He was that type of person, the one who worked first to know for himself.

AC: Do you have hope for real change here in Burma?

SUP: Resistance power is important for everyone. People work to develop physical resistance to withstand heat, cold, and fatigue. For the most part, people give priority to developing physical resistance. There's little concern for developing mental resistance. Of course, mental powers are also important. Nothing can be substituted for them. They can't be achieved by listening or reflecting alone. One has to work to develop them, to put focused energy into one's mind. When one has developed mental resistance power, one can withstand the ups and downs one encounters. When one encounters suffering, one can stand it. When one encounters happiness, one can stand it. Every time one experiences something good or bad, one doesn't get elated nor depressed. There is spiritual resistance, the strength to control one's mind. This is needed by everyone. It is weak in the world today. With the correct method it can be developed. There are spiritual faculties which bring self-control, self-mastery. These need to be developed in order to have spiritual resistance. They are called *indriya* or *bala* in Pali. For developing these faculties, the path of *satipaṭṭhāna* (practicing the four foundations of mindfulness) is best. One can't do this by meditating for just a short time. If one meditates meticulously, with real desire, one can gain these spiritual faculties. These faculties can be called spiritual multi-vitamins – similar to the multi-vitamins we take for physical health. When one develops the mind with *satipaṭṭhāna* meditation, this is like taking spiritual multi-vitamins. If half the world would possess these spiritual faculties in themselves the world would become peaceful.

The DHAMMA PROTECTS THOSE WHO PROTECT *the* DHAMMA.

..

ALAN CLEMENTS: Let's talk about extremism and religion in Myanmar. A short introduction to the question: Burma has been in the world's eye for some years, and especially now with the transfer of power to the new "National Reconciliation" government, as the National League for Democracy (NLD) calls it. The world is watching. They are celebrating, cautiously, as are the people of Burma. But, from all indications, it looks as though there is a miracle occurring, albeit a hard-earned one and only the first stage of a long and perhaps arduous process of reform.

So that the world will not think little of the *Buddha Sāsanā* in Myanmar, as an Elder in the *Sangha* (monastic order), what advice might you give to your fellow Buddhist monks, if they were in the room with us right now?

VENERABLE SAYADAW U PANDITA: What was your objective when you became a monk? The life of a monk is for liberation from the suffering of samsara (the beginning-less cycle of repeated birth, existence and dying again that all beings pass through). Just that. This objective should not be lost. If this objective isn't lost, you can do your work and carry out your duties. Is that objective being lost?

Self-protection is very important. A monk must make his ability to defend himself sturdy. He must practice to build his defense in advance.

There are two kinds protection: internal protection by means of internal suppression and external protection by means of external suppression.

The first kind of protection – inner protection – is to defend oneself against *lobha* (desire, selfishness), *dosa* (anger, cruelty, hatred) and *moha* (delusion, stupidity). These arise within one's being. If one gives in to these, under their influence one no longer behaves like a true human being. One cannot keep one's mentality humane. And although human, one loses one's basic human intelligence. This happens because one lacks the internal protection needed to overcome *lobha*, *dosa* and *moha* that arise from within. One should give priority to this internal protection.

One must make one's internal protection strong and sharp. One does this with the three trainings of *sīla* (moral integrity), *samādhi* (concentration) and *paññā* (liberating wisdom).[3] When one's internal protection becomes strong due to repeated practice, one will cherish their morality. The more one values their *sīla*, the more one will not allow it to weaken. One's ability to

---

3 The three trainings of *sīla*, *samādhi* and *paññā*, or morality, concentration and wisdom comprise the Dhamma, the teachings of the Buddha.

preserve it and make it strong will increase and become even stronger.

If the number of people who practice *sīla*, *samādhi* and *paññā* becomes large, the dhamma which they protect will protect them in return. In this way, there will be freedom from disturbances. When the practice of dhamma is not maintained, how can the dhamma protect a person?

In order to increase the number of people who practice *sīla*, *samādhi* and *paññā*, one must spread knowledge of the correct practice. During the time of the Buddha, people who professed the doctrine of self were the majority. The Buddha became enlightened in that environment. The Buddha understood for himself the doctrine of non-self, that there is no self, and taught the practical method for coming to understand this.

When there were more people like this, the disturbances they had didn't amount to much. And the *devas* gave their protection. They protect those who are doing good work.

Even our Buddha arose during a period when only one quarter of the people are good. This period is called *kali yūga*.[4] It is a time when peoples' behavior is for the most part quite immoral. Now, it has been more than 2,500 years since the passing away of the Buddha and the teachings of the Buddha have become very weak.

AC: You are aware that terrorism is an increasing problem all over the world. In my country of America, pretty much any western country for that matter, there's a deep and increasing fear of terrorism, whatever its ideological basis may be. My

---

4 There are four periods in time described in the texts. The worst is called *kali yuga*. *Kali yuga* means 'a period of many faults', a time where beings do many things wrong. If we look at the human population in the world and divide it into four parts, it is the period in time where only one part is good.

question: What advice might you offer to defeat radical extremism, that, I might add, in most cases considers success not only in the death of those whom they attack but in their own death, as well?

SUP: The best way is avoidance. Don't go to a place where there is fire. But if you can't avoid it, be prepared. Reasoning power is important. Reasoning power means there is *sātthaka sampajañña* and *sappāya sampajañña* (two of the four kinds of clear comprehension). The ability to weigh whether something one is about to do or say is beneficial or not is called *sātthaka sampajañña* (clear comprehension of benefit). One shouldn't do what is unbeneficial. Further, one should look to see if it is suitable or not. This is called *sappāya sampajañña* (clear comprehension of suitability). If something is both beneficial and suitable one should do it. Only then will one succeed. When one has reflected before acting or speaking many times, this knowledge becomes mature. Then it is easy in practice to avoid doing what is unbeneficial and unsuitable. This mature knowledge is called *pariharika paññā* (the wisdom to carry out what is both beneficial and suitable).[5] One becomes courageous about doing what is beneficial and suitable. When one avoids doing what is unbeneficial and unsuitable, then there is no detriment to oneself. And in doing what is beneficial and suitable, good results come.

For example, people need to consider before eating something, "Is this good for me or not? Is this suitable for me or not?" If it is suitable, when the time is right one should eat it. This is

---

5 *Pariharika paññā* is the combination of two of the four kinds of clear comprehension, clear comprehension of benefit and clear comprehension of suitability [*Sātthaka sampajañña* and *sappāya sampajañña*]. *Sampajañña*, or clear comprehension and *sampajāno*, someone who is clearly comprehending, are terms found in the *Mahā Satipaṭṭhāna Sutta*.

pariharika paññā: avoiding what is unbeneficial or unsuitable and carrying out what is both beneficial and suitable. This is very important for everyone. It is lacking in the world today.

AC: I was speaking with the American Ambassador not long ago about his views on the possible spread of violent extremism from abroad into Myanmar, and how disastrous that would be if it occurred. According to an alarming piece I read in a recent edition of the New Yorker Magazine, such ISIS-inspired activities are going on in neighboring Dhaka. What's required to raise the quality of governance in Burma to counter such a potential threat?

SUP: There are two programs for the country – a short-term program and a long-term program. The short-term program is to gather together as many elders and young adults as possible who know and have faith in the basic virtues of the *Buddha*, *Dhamma* and the *Sangha*, and are of good moral character. The long-term program is to train the children in basic Buddhist culture so that they will have good moral character as well as a good education. That is the long-term program for the country to become good again.

The long-term program is something like the example set by King Ashoka who ruled India in the 3rd century BC. At first he was violent and cruel. He ruled by the sword. He was hated by the people because he oppressed them. After meeting Buddhist monks who corrected him, he put down the sword and his cruelty and ruled by the *dhamma*.

He studied the Buddhist texts. He understood the precepts of a king, how to have *mettā* (loving-kindness) for the people and to handle things with foresight. Having studied the texts, he understood how to govern the people and how to support the teachings. Acting according to his understanding, during his reign the country became peaceful and the teachings flourished. He used the term *dhamma vijaya*, or "one who has gained personal victory with the *Dhamma* and the discipline."

He drew the conclusion that when the number of people who gain victory over themselves with the *dhamma* becomes large, it is easy to govern. That is the *Asoka* program. Later, so there would continue to be generations of good people, he built monasteries for learning the Buddhist scriptures and for practicing meditation. That is creating new generations.

'*Dhamma vijaya*' is the way to conquer oneself. If you conquer yourself, will you break your *sīla*? Or harm others?

The children who have been learning basic Buddhist culture at the centre are taught both theoretically and practically about the teachings of the Buddha. They also try to gain practical experience by meditating. The young people who have finished this program have formed a group called the *Dhamma Vijaya* youth group. These young people are using the method of King *Asoka*, even though they don't have his abilities yet. In the future they will be capable of good governance. This is the plan established for the long-term.

AC: Playing the devil's advocate, it's no longer just protecting ourselves from our inner enemies. In the world today there are real and lethal external dangers. So my question: do you see something required here to protect both the people and the *sāsana*, other than just mindfulness of one's own mind and one's protection against one's inner enemies?

SUP: There should be protection prepared in advance. It must be established. Combining theory and practice, one has to work to develop a large population with a firm commitment to the *dhamma*. Further, unity and harmony are very important.

One has to work to make oneself and one's group good. When one's group or community is good there will not be injustice towards others. When that attitude becomes mature, as it is said, *Dhammo have rakkhati dhammacārī* – the dhamma protects one who protects the dhamma, so as not to encounter danger nor to decline.

It's important to be able to defend oneself. In the *Parābhava Sutta*, the Buddha said, "*Dhammakāmo bhavaṃ hoti, Dhammadessī parābhavo.*" This means, 'One who learns the teaching and puts it into practice prospers. One who despises the teaching and the discipline declines.' When teaching the principles of Buddhist culture according to the instruction from the *Parābhava Sutta*, it is important for teachers, from elder Sayadaws on down to parents and schoolteachers, not just to teach the texts but to teach how theory is put into practice.

The teaching of the Buddha encourages self-protection by making SQ (spiritual intelligence or one's capacity for moral integrity, concentration, and wisdom) strong. If one can control oneself and gain self-victory, one will not feel troubled by others.

Which is more important, protection against external enemies or protection against internal enemies? Is it more important to conquer the external enemy, or the internal enemy?

AC: Well, it would depend on the circumstances. But I would say, the internal enemy. Even so, are you concerned that people of other religions will overwhelm Burma?

SUP: It can happen. People of other religions overwhelmed India, the place where Buddhism arose. When scriptural knowledge is not put into practice, a person doesn't know the benefits of the *Dhamma*. Not knowing its benefits, he doesn't value it. Not placing a value on the *Dhamma*, he won't try to preserve it, to keep it from disappearing. This is what is happening. A person needs to look at himself to see if the *Dhamma* has been lost or not. One has to work so that doesn't happen.

AC: In America, a pluralistic nation, there are many religions and spiritual faiths, as in Europe, Canada, Australia, and other democratic countries around the world. And the same here in Burma – all the major religions and faiths co-exist, albeit with stress and occasional bursts of violence. But what you're saying is that you think Burma will go the way of ancient India and lose its Buddhist culture?

SUP: If we can teach Buddhist cultural principles starting at a young age, the culture will take root in our children and become firm and strong. We have to take care with regard to preserving our own culture. But in preserving our culture, we must be careful not to harm others.

A plan needs to be established and carried out. If not, then within 50 years, at the very most 100 or 150 years, the teachings of the Buddha will leave the country of Myanmar.

AC: Some people have criticized Daw Aung San Suu Kyi for not defending Buddhism sufficiently enough here in Burma. When I have been asked about this in the media, I have, at times, pointed out that Daw Aung San Suu Kyi actively defends Buddhism, first, by being a nonviolent, sila-endowed practicing Buddhist who spent nearly 17 years under detention for her beliefs, both spiritual and political. But more to the point, when you look at the persecution of people here in Burma, the majority have been Buddhists. Of the thousands of people said to have been killed during the 1988 pro-democracy uprising, the vast majority were Buddhists. Of the additional 10,000 or more political prisoners that suffered in Burma's prisons, all but a few are Buddhists. Those tens-of-thousands forced into labor and portering for the military were mostly Buddhist. At the time of the Saffron Revolution here back in 2007, the military regime primarily focused on attacking Buddhist monks and monasteries and subsequently imprisoning and torturing many members of the Sangha. Overall, the Buddhists in Burma were the ones under siege by the former regime, by fellow Buddhists, at least, that's what they claim to be. And of course, the Karen and Kachin Christians and the Shans have also been under attack for many years.

SUP: Although they are nominally Buddhists, their understanding of the qualities of the *Buddha, Dhamma* and *Sangha* is vague, weak, deformed, without substance and totally uninformed. People who know nothing don't understand how to keep morality and the benefits of doing so. They don't understand the drawbacks incurred by immoral behavior. Thus they are not afraid to be immoral, commit misdeeds and be cruel. The good they do – making donations – has nothing to do with moral behavior.

AC: Few people know that you are Daw Aung San Suu Kyi's *dhamma* teacher. She looks to you for *dhamma* advice and guidance. If I am not mistaken, she learned meditation under house arrest from your book, *In This Very Life.* You receive her regularly. Her office often posts photographs on Facebook of your meetings; she's been here to Panditarama too many times to count. She's practiced meditation here. As such, you've paid a price for the association; from interrogation by MI (military intelligence); having the monastery's internet and electricity cut at times; being denied building permits and land use permits for branch monasteries; and many other ways as well. Throughout it, you have remained unscathed and steadfast – loyal in your association. You even have an NLD calendar featuring a large photograph of Daw Suu on the wall here in your meeting room.

With that said, would you care to comment about the criticisms leveled at her?

SUP: I can't be everywhere, going after all those people. "What you do is the work at hand, where you get to [at night] is where you make camp." When planting rice or beans, farmers choose a place with fertile soil. Only then will their work be worthwhile. If one ignores the workable land one has and goes and plants on untilled, virgin land, what good will it do? One should do what works.

I ask you. To whom would you give priority, if both were to approach you at the same time: a person with good potential or a person with little potential?

AC: The first person.

SUP: Right. Choosing is important.

It is no good to try to become a hero by means that don't pacify hatred but only increase it. Daw Aung San Suu Kyi has become a heroine by pacifying quarrels according to the way of the Buddha. She didn't try to become a heroine, but she has become one naturally.

There is a Burmese saying, *follow the example of Asoka.* We spoke about him earlier. King Asoka ruled in India more than 2,000 years ago. Wielding the power of the sword, he ruled with cruelty so that people had no room to move. They had no freedom. And the people hated him. He was known as "Cruel Asoka." Later, when he put down the sword and ruled according to the *dhamma,* he became successful.

Government can only work after one has gained victory over oneself by means of the *dhamma.* King Asoka was the first to use the term, '*dhamma vijaya,*' or '*victory by means of the dhamma.*'

In particular, the people at all levels of government, if their administration is to be effective, should conquer themselves by means of the dhamma, not just superficially but with right practice. Asoka also worked to enable the people to gain dhamma victory for themselves. He became very successful. H. G. Wells said much in praise of Asoka, saying there had never been anyone like him before. ("... the name of Asoka shines, and shines almost alone, a star." The Outline of History, 1920).

When he ruled by the sword, he was known as 'Cruel Asoka,' but after he put down the sword and began to rule by the *dhamma*, he became very successful and was known as 'Righteous Asoka [*Dhammasoka*].' Those who govern should always look back at history.

If you can't overcome the internal enemies, they not only give you trouble but give others trouble too. And in future lives they also give trouble. An ordinary, external enemy can't debase you. If he or she kills you, it's only in one lifetime. The internal enemies kill a being lifetime after lifetime. They also degrade one. They are quite frightening.

AC: Thank you Sir.

The DHAMMA *of* RECONCILIATION
and the SQ REVOLUTION

..

ALAN CLEMENTS: I would like to follow up with the issue of "National Reconciliation" – the centerpiece of (Myanmar State Counsellor) Daw Aung San Suu Kyi and her government's vision of a peaceful and prosperous Burma. Obviously, this is an epic challenge. Would you share your thoughts on overcoming those forces within oneself – those defilements – that prevent genuine reconciliation with those who have harmed us? Your guidance would not only be a gift to the people of your country but the world over. As we know, conflicts are everywhere, and if we expect to overcome them, we need urgent wise leadership. We need both a moral compass and the ethical courage, and the "spiritual intelligence" or the mindful intelligence, to make real on Daw Aung San Suu Kyi's hope of a healed nation. What happens here may serve as a model for peace everywhere.

What is the *dhamma* of reconciliation?

VENERABLE SAYADAW U PANDITA: As far as Daw Aung San Suu Kyi's side goes, they are ready. The previous government abused our country and the people. They are at fault, and if they admit those acts, everything will work out. As I said before, just as monks do when they commit a monastic offense, if they admit honestly and bravely, "We simply acted according to how we saw things, but, as everyone knows, this is what came about; we take full responsibility, these acts are our fault," then everything will work out.

Human beings should have the courage to avoid doing what is wrong and the courage to do and to say what is beneficial. If one does something wrong, whether deliberately or out of carelessness, one needs to have the courage to admit one's mistake.

The Pali word *vīriya* means the courage to avoid doing things that are wrong, the courage to do what is right and if one errs, the courage to admit it. That is called *vīriya*. When taking such a moral risk, one must bear the suffering encountered. Such courage must be nurtured. It does not come quickly. You must develop it gradually.

When the courage to refrain from doing wrong becomes strong, one will understand that they are free of fault. One will also have the courage to do things that are good. When one does good things, good results will come. When one knows what is beneficial and free of fault, one will value the ability to take risks. When the attitude of valuing courage arises in the mind, one won't allow one's courage to decline.

Firstly, there must be honesty. The difficulty is that few people are honest. Because of dishonesty, there's much deceit.

You were formerly a monk. When you commit an offense, what must you do?

AC: Admit it openly in front of the *Sangha*.

SUP: Right, you have to admit it. First of all, you have to avoid committing an offense, but if you know you have committed one, you must confess it.

In the realm of *dhamma*, whether one is a monk, nun, or a lay person, there are rules and responsibilities. Lay people have their rules and responsibilities, monks have their rules and duties, and nuns have theirs. When one knows these rules and duties and acts accordingly, it's like keeping to your lane when traveling. One automatically goes in the right direction.

It won't do to learn these duties and responsibilities only when one becomes an adult. They need to be learned from a young age. Just as one must try to make one's IQ good, at the same time one must also try to make one's SQ (spiritual intelligence) good. It won't do to make SQ good only after one's IQ has become good. It's just like feeding a child appropriately. You must first nurse the baby and then all along the way, gradually, feed the child appropriately, taking into account the child's age, size, growth and of course, both the quantity and quality of the food. Good health has many considerations. But you must feed the child appropriately starting from a young age.

Parents have the first duty to teach the child and after them, teachers have their duty to teach them. In the world there are many parents and many teachers who do not fulfill their duties. This is, in large part, why the world is in such conflict and being destroyed. Have you thought about it?

AC: I have, especially as a parent.

SUP: For the world to be peaceful, parents are crucial because they are a child's first teachers. Even in Myanmar where Buddhism flourishes, because there are so many people who are ill-equipped to be parents, the *dhamma* has declined. Because I knew that many parents were not fulfilling their responsibilities, since the days of Mahasi Yeiktha I've tried to teach children about Buddhist culture both in theory and practice, so that a new generation could emerge. This was a priority and remains so.

AC: Can you say more about nurturing courage?

SUP: Parents have to explain this to their children so that they develop the courage to avoid doing what is wrong. An analogy is that parents should explain the bad results of eating what is unsuitable for them. To avoid eating food which is not suitable requires courage. When one courageously avoids unsuitable food, one doesn't suffer.

Similarly, parents should explain the benefits of eating suitable and appropriate food. Eating suitable food also requires courage. If one has courage, one gains benefits such as good digestion, physical energy, healthiness, and so on.

Parents should explain the value of having courage to avoid doing wrong and to do what is right by using comparisons like this that children can understand. This will only come about through establishing a specific plan. It can't be done without one.

In America, a country where science and technology flourish, education or IQ has been given great emphasis, whereas moral behavior and emotional intelligence or EQ have been ignored. Proceeding in this way, children gain a worldly education but there are many teenagers who have become immoral. Searching for the cause, one can draw the conclusion that it is because moral behavior is being ignored.

In a research study it was found that a person's success was due to IQ in only 25% of the people studied, while EQ was crucial to success in 75% of those studied. Afterwards, EQ became the first priority and IQ the second.

Because our country is doing the same as America – emphasizing IQ over moral behavior – teenagers are becoming immoral. Therefore, in our (*dhamma*) courses for children I emphasize SQ (spiritual intelligence) in order to strengthen it in them. I use the term SQ in place of EQ. SQ (spiritual intelligence) stands for *sīla* (ethical intelligence) and *sikkhā* for training[6]. And the highest is *satipaṭṭhāna* (cultivating the four foundations of mindfulness). All three words begin with 'S.'

When Daniel Goleman, who popularized the term EQ (emotional intelligence), came to speak with me, I told him I prefer to use the term 'SQ' (spiritual intelligence). He agreed and concluded that people with good SQ are able to skillfully assess themselves. They know what sort of person they are. That's the first quality. They are able to control their impulses.

In America, there is a lot of tension, stress, and depression. People with good SQ are able to control these feelings. They are able to maintain their discipline. In SQ, this refers to the five precepts. Further, they have compassion for others. They also feel gladdened by others' good characteristics. They aren't jealous or envious. When something must be done, they have the intelligence to evaluate whether it is beneficial or not and whether it is suitable or not.

We should give priority to SQ and de-emphasize IQ. This is in keeping with the teaching of the Buddha, to teach children right from wrong, then provide an education.

It's been more than 50 years that I have been teaching this program to the children, since my days at Mahasi Yeiktha. This program is the basic Buddhist culture course for children. It's

---

6 The three-fold training in higher virtue (*adhisīla-sikkhā*), higher mind (*adhicitta-sikkhā*), and higher wisdom (*adhipaññā-sikkhā*).

a training in SQ. In essence, the children are taught, "Those things are bad and they bring bad results." Knowing that something is wrong, one shouldn't fail in one's duty to avoid it. "Those things are good." Knowing what is good, one shouldn't fail in one's duty to undertake them. Not neglecting to avoid what should be avoided and doing what should be done. That is called *appamāda*, or heedfulness.

AC: Then the question arises, how to get parents to wake up and bring their children to Panditarama, and to understand the value of SQ?

SUP: Parents have woken up – they know and they accept that their own children know more than they do about the teachings of the Buddha. They are alert to this. Over the last 50 years [in Myanmar], most parents failed in their duties to their children. Teachers, for the most part, failed in their duties to their students. They have come to realize their failure. But it's just a small oasis in a vast, burning desert. And in comparison with the whole world, it's a tiny spot.

AC: To actualize reconciliation and abide in clear conscience, you speak of the necessity of having the courage to honestly admit one's mistakes. But as a former monk, before ordination, I was aware of the rules expected of me and agreed to follow them. And if I failed to keep any one of them, I also agreed – out of self-honor and respect for the *Sangha*, as well as the lay people who supported us – to openly admit my failings.

In Myanmar and her quest for National Reconciliation, we have people – the oppressors, the old guard – who have made no such commitment to a moral code of conduct or rule of law. To the contrary, the majority of them, perhaps all of them, so it seems, think they've done the right thing for the country. So the idea of admitting a mistake when they in fact think their actions were not only justified but were for the betterment of the people, blind as that may be, is essentially asking one to admit to something they do not see in themselves. Or do they, and they are pretending? Of course, only they know.

Regardless, if courage is required to admit one's wrongdoing, how to get someone, who doesn't see that what they did was wrong, to actually admit that what they did violated others? In other words, how to overcome self-deception?

SUP: Just look back on your own life and the things you do every day, whether doing something for yourself or for others. It's never perfect. There are times when something is missing, when something is lacking or especially when something is wrong. The Buddha talked about these three things: the gaps, the things that are needed and the things that are off, incorrect. He also talked about how to fill in the gaps, how to complete the parts that are incomplete, and how to make things correct. It's very important to be able to look back and see that. When you look at your own life and then you see, "Oh! This is missing," that's admitting your error. You ask, "Is there something lacking here, in this task?" When you recognize that something is lacking, that's admitting your fault. "I did these things incorrectly, they're not right – I missed the mark." One has to understand that. If there is an error, one has to look for the reason and correct it.

A person's life is like driving a car. When driving one must stay in one's lane, right? If one starts to swerve out of one's lane, one has to correct this and straighten out. To be able to steer is essential. This ability to steer is called *yoniso manasikāra* (wise consideration).

The same can be said with a boat, you always have to control the rudder. And in order to steer well, you must learn how. But for the most part, people cannot control their own lives. They're without the ability to steer. Although they have a rudder, they can't steer. Do you think that's true?

AC: Sure, there's chaos everywhere. It's rather maddening, frankly. But this madness has become normalized, in many ways. And often, those who point out this madness – those who can't steer, as you know from having lived under totalitarian regimes for over fifty years – are often considered mad and scapegoated, vilified, even imprisoned. As was Daw Aung San Suu Kyi and many of her NLD colleagues, and for decades. What was lacking in their oppressors, besides being unable to properly steer their lives?

SUP: When they were young, their parents didn't teach them properly.

AC: Bad parenting?

SUP: That's right. Because the parents were lacking, because they did not fulfill their responsibilities. Look at the *Singālovāda Sutta*, in the *Pātika Vagga* of the *Dīgha Nikāya*. This explains six sets of human relationships in society and shows what responsibilities or duties people have to each other, how they should relate to each other.

AC: You mentioned, 'when one takes risks, one must be able to bear the suffering encountered.' Would you shed light on how to ignite one's conscience to say something as radical as, "I ordered the killing of your brother, I ordered the torture of your daughter, I steered our country down a road of ruin and created a authoritarian state. And in so doing, I amassed an enormous amount of wealth and at your expense. And I did it because I was driven by fear and extreme selfish greed. Now, I humbly stand before you with shame. How can I make my wrongs right?"

SUP: First of all, there has to be the courage to avoid doing wrong. Daw Aung San Suu Kyi has this. If she does something wrong, she knows it. People who always have mindfulness know, "I've made a mistake," when they have erred. When correct, they know that too. When in error, they correct the mistake. When correct, they simply keep on going straight ahead. Like driving a car.

AC: That's for oneself, but what about for others?

SUP: If one can control oneself, others are automatically preserved, because one doesn't do harm. She understands that too. Self-control is not just for one's own benefit. It's not just for one's own physical, verbal and mental behavior. To the extent one controls oneself, one no longer harms others and one protects others so that they aren't harmed. There are two methods for this. There is self-control because one has moral shame and moral fear of doing wrong, and self-control because one understands how others would feel if harmed. However, it may be, both sides benefit. The difficulty is that most people do not have these qualities.

AC: For decades, the previous regimes did not see their errors. When people don't see their faults how can there be National Reconciliation and a peaceful, united country?

SUP: They're like a boat, the bow of which is broken and can't be maneuvered. So instead of trying to fix them, the only thing to do is gather people together who are in agreement and work to make yourself and the country good. If one pays attention to those people, how will anything be accomplished?

AC: Unify like minds?

SUP: It's very important to get the work done.

AC: How would you define the 'work' to be done?

SUP: Human beings have what are called moral behavior and duty. First and most important is moral behavior and after that, duty or responsibility. It's very important to fulfill these two. If one has been born a human being, then one should have the courage to ask, "What morals do I need to be a true human being?" If one investigates, one will come to understand morality. Next, you must put it into practice. If one doesn't know one's duties, one needs to learn them and fulfill them. When those two things are fulfilled – good moral behavior and our human responsibilities – one becomes a true human being.

It's also important to keep your mind humane, to keep your mind like a human's mind should be. You can't just look at what benefits you. You've got to look at what's good for others, too. You have to do what is good for others as much as possible, and do it with an attitude of goodwill.

One should also have compassion, the feeling of wanting to respond to the needs of others. When there is a basic attitude of *mettā* (goodwill) and *karunā* (compassion) there won't be envy for others' good circumstances. Rather, there will be the desire for others to enjoy the good circumstances one has for oneself; *muditā* (sympathetic joy) will arise. These are basic mental attitudes of a true human being.

Further, human beings encounter two kinds of things – good and bad. We experience good things and bad things. We encounter things that we like and we encounter things that we do not like. Things which are depressing and things to be happy about. In the face of these things, we shouldn't react. We should nurture equanimity, or balance of mind. The more we nurture this attitude, every time we encounter something good or bad, we won't respond with liking or rejection, but will remain balanced, in equanimity.

For this, *sātthaka sampajañña* and *sappāya sampajañña*, or reasoning power which is able to consider whether something is beneficial or unbeneficial, and suitable or unsuitable, is very important.

In particular, when one practices the *dhamma* consistently and knows the true *dhamma* to a large extent, the mind matures. When the mind matures, it has resistance power. Physical stamina is the ability to withstand the punishment of heat, cold, fatigue, and so on. When the mind gains knowledge, it becomes mature. Due to being mature, although the mind encounters something good, it doesn't feel elated. Similarly, when encountering something bad, it doesn't get depressed. It is able to stay balanced in between elation and depression. This is called equanimity. It's important to gain this ability.

Look at your own life. Before you practiced meditation, before you gained knowledge of the *dhamma*, what was your life like? And after practicing, what was your life like then? Do you see the changes before and after practicing?

AC: Yes, I've seen dramatic changes; nothing short of miraculous.

SUP: This is like being reborn in this very life.

AC: Beautiful!

SUP: This is the only way to be reborn without dying. One's life changes for the better due to the practice, not for the worse.

AC: Yes, meditation changed my life.

SUP: When something is this valuable, why do so few people pursue it?

AC: Well, you have to be smart. You have to see life and death and the limitations of sense pleasure and the emptiness of desire. You must become weary of the ego and tired of the *kilesas*, attachment, addictions, and fear. And even if you have wealth or success, you have to be smart enough to see them as a house of cards or a sand castle; conditions beyond your control and changing all the time. And further, it takes a lot of effort to turn inward, to seek a higher inner refuge, a higher freedom born from insight into *dhamma.*

SUP: When you want something valuable, you have to pay the price. Faith, effort, mindfulness and concentration, or *saddhā, viriya, sati,* and *samādhi,* are the price.

AC: Earlier, you encouraged reconciliation through cultivating the compassion practice of putting oneself into another person's place and feeling how they might be feeling. Would you share more on this process? I think most good people would like to be more compassionate: abandon egoism, discrimination, any hint of apartheid.

SUP: Has it ever happened that someone yelled at you, cursed you?

AC: Yes. I've encountered my fair share of abusive people.

SUP: Can you bear it? And do you like it?

AC: I did not like it. I found it revolting.

SUP: What you don't like, others wouldn't like either. The ability to put ourselves in another person's place is based upon the ability to reason. It's called empathy, or consideration for others. People who are selfish do not have that ability to reason, to reflect like that.

AC: What is this state of consciousness, the ability to reflect?

SUP: Reasoning power, or what is called clear comprehension of benefit and suitability (*sātthaka sampajañña* and *sappāya sampajañña*). It's what we discussed earlier. People do not have the ability to think about what is beneficial and suitable for others if they are only thinking about themselves.

AC: Consideration for others, the requisite of a great leader?

SUP: Yes, it's important for a leader to have that quality.

AC: If there's reconciliation and harmony in Parliament, there'll be harmony in the country. Maybe it should be advocated, that there should be an SQ retreat. Should the MPs go on retreat?

SUP: That would be the best.

AC: And maybe for the military as well.

SUP: In India, at the time of the Buddha, King Bimbisāra ruled the country after becoming a *sotāpañña* (the first stage of enlightenment). And, while continuing his *dhamma* practice under the Buddha's guidance, he also continued to fulfill the duties of his office. The world cannot be ruled by weapons and administrative power alone. There must be this justice of the *Dhamma* to rule the world. That's why, in the old days when kings ruled their countries, they were known as '*Dhammiko*,' a *dhamma* person or '*Dhammarājā*,' a king who rules with *dhamma*.

AC: This is the military version of SQ?

SUP: There should never be unjust killing or oppression. But a person who leads the country needs to be precise in following the laws. That is the ruler's duty.

AC: Sayadaw-gyi, I appreciate your reasoning power, your discerning wisdom, your warrior-like expression of spiritual intelligence. And I pray that your *dhamma* advice serves to facilitate reconciliation and peace-building both here in Myanmar and around the world. I am honored that you share it. Thank you.

SUP: This is just the way the Buddha taught.

LOOKING *for the* DHAMMA
YOU FIND IT IN YOURSELF.

..

ALAN CLEMENTS: I would like to thank you once again for taking the time to share your wisdom, both for the people of your country and others around the world. Tonight, I would like to follow up with issues raised in our previous conversations. You have shared quite a lot on the reconciling process. You've also touched upon SQ (spiritual intelligence) as foundational wisdom for enacting that process. We've talked about healing the wounds between the oppressed and the oppressors as a means of fostering peace and harmony among the people. We've also talked about good parenting - the importance of parents knowing their duties to their children and doing them well.

My question: Burma is the newest born democracy on earth. We have several hundred new members of parliament, cabinet members, ministers, a new president and vice presidents, and most of them have never before been in positions of high-leadership. In fact, many of them spent the majority of the past two decades as prisoners of conscience, here in their own country.

Would you speak about the *dhamma* qualities of good leadership?

VENERABLE SAYADAW U PANDITA: In order to understand what qualities a good leader needs to have in terms of the *dhamma*, first of all, we have to look at the qualities of a good friend, a *kalyāṇa mitta*. There are six qualities this person should have:

- *Piya* – to have good personal behavior, not just pretending. When one has good personal behavior, one is loved by those around one. This is the first quality that needs to be mentioned.

- Not only does the person have good personal behavior, they have a good mental attitude and are able to help others. Due to this, the person receives the respect of others. There must also be this quality of being respected, called *garu*.

- These two qualities combined lead to *bhāvaniya*, which means to be the recipient of others' *mettā* (loving kindness).

- The next quality is *vattā*, which means when there is something to be said that is beneficial and true, the person can speak frankly.

- Further, when they receive criticism from others, they can accept it. This is called *vacanakkhama*.

- And the last quality is that they do not use those who depend on them inappropriately – *no c'aṭṭhāne niyujjako*. This means not urging people who depend on you to do things for your benefit that aren't good for them to do; not to use people for your own selfish means.

A person who possesses these six qualities is a good friend, or *kalyāna mitta*. One has to start by understanding this. That is what the Buddha taught. If a person possesses these qualities, one could choose that person as a friend, mentor or a teacher.

AC: These six qualities of a *kalyāna mitta* also apply to good leadership?

SUP: Yes. It's important to possess the qualities of a good friend.

AC: How can one know and trust that a person has these attributes?

SUP: In human society, if someone has good morality, or good personal behavior, those around that person will come to perceive this. Associate and you'll know. Over time, one comes to know through association with another whether they have a bad character or a good character. But, one can't find this out in a short time. One must take time to choose a good person.

There are six other qualities of a good leader. First of all, leaders must be patient (*khamā*), in all ways. They must be able to bear heat, cold, suffering, and blame from others. That's important. Second, *jāgariya*: they must be watchful, vigilant and prompt to act. And *utthāna*, they must be active. Fourth, *samvibhāga*: they should share what they have with friends and associates, and not just keep things for themselves. Five, they should have compassion for others (*karunā*). Six, *ikkhana* or foresight: they should be able to assess a situation accurately. If a person has these six qualities, one could choose that person as a good friend, a teacher or a leader. Here, the text refers to a leader of the *Sangha*, but anyone who is a leader of an organization or association should have these qualities.

AC: What is another word for foresight?

SUP: Foresight can also be called reasoning power; when there is something to be done, it is the ability to consider whether that task is beneficial or not. If it is beneficial, then to consider further whether it is suitable or not. And whether or not the time is right to do it. What is important is that one's actions should not be detrimental for oneself or for others. Even though you may not be able to help, you can control yourself so that you don't bother others. There is a Burmese proverb, *"If you can't help, let it be, but don't make trouble."*

AC: In reference to having consideration for another and then through reasoning power determining what would be beneficial or harmful to that person, and from there, acting appropriately, what if 'the other' is not yet born – we are going forward here a generation or two; can you speak to that type of future-reaching foresight, or multi-generational compassion, that exchanges self for others not yet born?

This question is more relevant today than ever, as many leaders in our world have not had the foresight nor the compassion to see the effects of what looked to be a wise decision in their day, but as it turned out, was detrimental to future generations. For example, nuclear power and nuclear weapons have placed life in jeopardy; they hold all life hostage. In addition, we have a 'homicidal economy' fueled by obsessive consumption and the blind burning of fossil fuels, that has led to global warming, runaway climate change, and with it, the melting of the polar caps and the release of toxic methane, and the acidification of the oceans, habitat loss and disruption of food supplies, and the possibility of extinction, perhaps much sooner than we think. All based on human ignorance – the absence of reasoning and the obsession with "self, progress, and stuff." And all done, for the most part, by so-called educated leaders trying their best to do what was right for the people. But, it's been the very opposite of foresight and far-reaching compassion. Few people were able to think that far ahead; few people were able to put themselves in the shoes of the unborn and determine what was best for them.

The question: how to really know what it means to put one-self in the mind of Life not yet conceived? What does it mean to embody future generations and have the foresight to care for those life-forms, the animals, the birds, the trees, the water, the people, all life, known and unknown? This is an essential question, in part, because Burma is the latest birth of democracy on the planet and the learning that has gone on in older democracies could be made here with good intentions, yet without the foresight to sustain in the long term.

Translator: Alan is saying that because some of the present leaders of the world don't have vision or foresight, for example, the destruction of species, the destruction of forests, the natural disasters that are now occurring, the disruption of the order of things, cutting down forests to an extreme, extreme use of petroleum, are things that were done because of a lack of reasoning and foresight. Due to this, there are all kinds of problems in the world now. The extinction of species, about 200 a day, for example. At present, they are even trying to find types of fuel other than petroleum, ways to avoid global warming and pollution. Because of a lack of vision, all over the world people are encountering all sorts of problems. If the leaders of the future were to have this type of vision regarding future generations, how would you advise them, in terms of *dhamma*?

SUP: That would be difficult. When there is selfishness, when people are self-centered, and all that matters is getting what they want, or what their group wants, when people are oppressed by greed, then *mettā* and *karunā* have dried up. One no longer cares for the welfare of others. One no longer knows how to have love and compassion for others, whether presently alive or future generations. As a result, their duties as humans are left unfulfilled.

In the world today, selfishness – a lack of *mettā* and a lack of *karuṇā* – are thick. People are human in form, but not truly human. And there is no truth, no foresight, no compassion, no ability to truly see what is beneficial for others and have the courage to do what is right and refrain from what is wrong. People no longer know there is truth, and that they should stand by what is true.

AC: Standing by the truth?

SUP: What this means is that there is a correct, straight path – 'That's right.' If one approaches a *kalyāṇa mitta* and has the ability to weigh whether something is beneficial or not, whether something is suitable or not, the quality of being upright and pure, *uju*, arises. Because one comes to know what is beneficial and correct, the quality of being upright, or *uju*, comes to be. Then people are able to keep their own discipline – keep their *sīla*. People should be moral and fulfill their duties. This is important. If one doesn't keep basic morality and doesn't perform the duties and responsibilities that one should perform, because of no longer understanding the benefits of doing this, then the upright, pure mind will not arise. Therefore, one must explain to others the importance of morality as well as encourage an understanding of their social responsibilities. Then one must be watchful to see if they do as explained. Do they keep their morality or not? Do they fulfill their duties or not?

As one waits and sees, if they do things sincerely, is there benefit or not? When people can see that they are gaining benefit, then restraint will follow. People will feel, "Because we respect this path, things are peaceful and beneficial. When our morality is good and we fulfill our duties and responsibilities, good things come." Because they understand the benefits, they are sure to follow straight along this path.

There are people who kill others, who steal, who commit adultery or other sexual offenses, who lie, who take drugs and intoxicants and go wild because of them. One realizes that it is good to avoid these actions. One realizes, "If I avoid doing these things, my behavior becomes clean, my morality is intact and other people are not harmed because of what I do." This is an upright mental attitude. When one really looks at this, one comes to realize that it's peaceful. One's morality is intact, and it's good for others too. When one sees this, one doesn't want to lose the benefits one has developed. One is sure to walk along this straight path.

When people who initially don't know anything about the *dhamma* practice and come to know the nature of the *dhamma*, what happens? Is their mind the same after they practice, as it was before? It's not the same any more, it changes, doesn't it? It's like that.

If one hasn't yet made oneself upright with correct means, then one does not have any confidence in doing it because the results haven't yet appeared. In that case, one will just keep going along one's way. One's path won't be straight. But when one realizes the benefits, one will go straight.

In essence, one has to first learn the method for developing self-control so one doesn't follow the wrong path, so that one can keep from doing things that are wrong. When one has a reliable method, one simply follows that correct path. Following the correct path, one reaches a safe place. Because one has learned the method for self-control and one knows the benefits of gaining self-control, as well as the faults of not gaining self-control, one will surely control oneself. And being free of fault, one experiences good results. When one can restrain oneself, problems are sure to be solved.

For solving these problems, in order to get the best answer, now and for the future, practice *satipaṭṭhāna* to a satisfactory level. Before practicing *satipaṭṭhāna* and after practicing *satipaṭṭhāna*, how did your life change?

AC: In every way.

SUP: Was it a good change? Did you gain self-mastery?

AC: I certainly improved, nothing short of miraculous.

SUP: So, you have the answer.

AC: On the subject of *satipaṭṭhāna*, this next question is universal, in that it applies to everyone and has the potential to benefit all beings in this world, now and in the future. I think it was Burma's first Prime Minister, U Nu, who was, as you know, one of the founders of Mahasi Yeiktha here in Yangon – where the worldwide mass lay mindfulness movement began – who said, over fifty or so years ago, that Burma's number one export was mindfulness.

Prophetically, he was right. Mindfulness is now a global phenomenon and a lucrative one as well. Fortune Magazine recently reported it to be a $1-billion-dollar industry. And I'm sure you are aware that mindfulness training is being applied in numerous multi-billion dollar corporations; Ford, Google, American Express, to name just a few.

Pro-athletes espouse it as the basis of their expertise. We see it being taught in prisons. In hospitals. Colleges. High schools. Even children, as in Burma, are seeing its tremendous benefits; increasing their ability to focus, reduce their stress and anxiety, and better able to manage negative emotions.

We also see mindfulness being used in the military. I'm not sure how deep into the military it's applied, but when we use the word military, we generally mean both defense and offense. So it's probably being used anywhere from combat, to stress management in highly volatile areas and I wouldn't be surprised if it's used by those who pilot drones from a safe distance that strike thousands of miles away and either kill their intended targets and or kill innocent civilians.

At 95 years old you are perhaps the most Elder Buddhist monk in Myanmar. Having ordained at age of 12, with a tremendous knowledge, both theoretically and experientially, of the *satipaṭṭhāna dhamma*, you are perhaps the senior-most teacher of mindfulness in the world, with tens of thousands of students both in Myanmar and worldwide.

I think it is fair to say, that the majority of people who currently practice it and guide others in it, have little idea that its origins are rooted in Buddhism and *dhamma*, or, perhaps, that there's an entire culture here in Myanmar that has been practicing *sati* (mindfulness) for centuries.

My question: would you care to offer a few points of guidance to anyone interested in pursuing the practice of mindfulness or more specifically the practice of *satipaṭṭhāna*, especially as it becomes more embedded worldwide?

SUP: What's most important is to find a good spiritual friend, a *kalyāṇa mitta* and practice meditation. There are seven qualities that a good spiritual friend must have as explained in the *Visuddhimagga*, which quotes what the Buddha taught. The seven qualities are: being loved (*piya*), being respected (*garu*), being the object of others' *mettā* (*bhāvaniya*), being able to say frankly to the students what they need to hear (*vattā*), being able to take it when others criticize them (*vacanakkhama*), being able to speak about the deep *dhamma* because of both practice and understanding the theory (*gambhirañca katham kattā*), and not using one's students in inappropriate ways, for one's own benefit (*no c'aṭṭhāne niyujjako*).

The qualities of *piya, garu, bhāvaniya* and so on are resultant qualities. In order to possess them, one must possess the causal qualities: *saddhā, sīla, sūta, cāga, vīriya, sati, samādhi* and *paññā* (faith, morality, learning, generosity, effort, mindfulness, concentration and wisdom). When a person has these causal qualities, they don't have to say, "May others love me." It automatically happens that such people are loved and that they're also worthy of respect. People have the feeling of wanting such a person to be well and happy. A person with such qualities is brave enough to speak when there's something that needs to be said, and when other people criticize them, they can forbear and be patient. Because one has practiced the *dhamma* of *satipaṭṭhāna* to a satisfactory level one is able to speak about the profound *dhamma*. And possessing the courage to avoid doing what is wrong and to undertake what is correct, one doesn't use one's students inappropriately.

This is how to look at a teacher, in terms of those qualities. You should examine if a person is a true *kalyāṇa mitta*, a good spiritual friend possessed of these qualities. This is what the Buddha taught. Why? Because one has to choose a good guide in order to take the right path. Only then will one go the right way.

The Buddha said that *sati* (mindfulness) is needed everywhere. He acknowledged this in the word *sabbatthika* – *sati* is needed everywhere, like fresh air. We need air every second, don't we? If we breathe polluted air, immediately we feel tight and tense and if we breathe air that contains poison we can die immediately. *Sati* is needed everywhere. It's like fresh air. Think about it.

People usually don't think breathing fresh air is important. Or it's not a big deal. But if you think about it, it's not only important, it's essential. And it's something we must do immediately, right now. If we don't breathe we die.

You have to do it right now; you have to do it repeatedly; you have to do it in time; and you need to breathe fresh air. That is why people may not necessarily think that breathing fresh air is important or don't even think about breathing as something that's important because it's happening all the time. But you have to do it yourself. You have to do it right away, right now. You have to do it regularly. And if you do that, the results are good for you. These four aspects are important.

In the same way one applies mindfulness. You need to do it yourself; you have to do it right now; you have to do it regularly; and the results will be beneficial. Every important thing that a person does has these four characteristics. You can look at anything in terms of those four points and if it has those four characteristics, you know it is one of the most important things you can do: that you cannot not do it, you have to do it yourself, you have to do it regularly and in time, and it is very beneficial.

AC: What are your thoughts about teaching *sati* (mindfulness) removed from *satipaṭṭhāna*? Is it still effective? Can you be deluded about thinking it's effective? And are there dangers in teaching from that separation?

What I mean by 'separation', is removing the Buddhist context from *sati*, removing the ontological eco-system from the root concept of mindfulness. In other words, teaching mindfulness without reference to *dhamma*, Buddhism, *nāma-rūpa*, the five aggregates, the progress of insight, awareness of *anicca*, *anatta* and *dukkha,* or the four foundations of mindfulness, or the eight-fold path, or the four noble truths, or the seven factors of enlightenment or *nibbāna;* purposely removing the key transformational constructs of the *dhamma,* the Buddha's teaching, from it. So by removing the *dhamma* from *sati,* I'm assuming one is removing *satipaṭṭhāna* from it and teaching mindfulness as a stand-alone state of mind.

Further, there's a tremendous debate in the West and perhaps the world, on what the 'mindful' state of mind really is. There doesn't seem to be a clear consensus on the true nature of mindfulness.

SUP: As the Buddha said, *"Sati* is needed everywhere." In the olden days, there was a monk who was given the instruction to rub a small piece of cloth – just to keep on rubbing it with awareness. While rubbing the cloth, *vīriya* (energy), *sati* (mindfulness), and *samādhi* (concentration) arose, and he became enlightened.

If we look at this from a modern-day perspective, it seems laughable – not something an adult would do. But as the monk was rubbing, his mind became concentrated. At first, insight-knowledge didn't arise. But later, he came to know 'touching.' He rubbed, and knew the 'rubbing.' *Samādhi* arose, then there was touching, and knowing the touching. These moments of touching and knowing arose and then disappeared. He came to know the arising and passing away (of the mental and physical phenomena). *Vipassanā* (insight) knowledge arose. None of the teachings of the Buddha were mentioned, just to rub the cloth – the 'doctrine' of rubbing.

AC: So, mindfulness is sufficient in itself to free the mind? That when practiced rightly, mindfulness reveals reality, and as such, awakens insight into the arising and passing of phenomena, and freedom follows?

SUP: It is not a matter of 'practicing mindfulness rightly.' Reality is revealed when there is focus on the object, *sati* becomes steadfast and doesn't separate from the object but always stays with it.

AC: And what stays with the object is mindfulness? What is the object – seeing, hearing, smelling and so on?

SUP: It could be any of these, as long as one is observing real mental and physical qualities as they arise.

A person learning to shoot at a target must aim. There's a target with a bull's eye. One has to aim and then shoot. So that mental defilements, *kilesas*, won't arise, we aim at the arising object. When *sati* is established on the object it doesn't give *kilesas* the chance to arise. When I am sitting in a chair that is big enough for only one person, no one else can sit here. It's the same when *sati* is established on the object.

If *kilesas* do arise, then what to do? Note them accurately and in a focused way.

This is like prevention and cure. One protects against the enemy, but if the enemy comes one notes it immediately. So, when the object arises we need effort and aiming, or *viriya* and *vitakka*. Aiming is like placing the object in our sight and effort is like pulling the trigger.

We note the main object of the rising and falling of the abdomen, don't we? We put our mind on the abdomen, like waiting to greet a visitor. As soon as the abdomen rises, the observing mind must be there. We must have ardent effort – *ātāpa* – as well as accurate aim. These, first of all, are the most important things. Because when they are present *sati* and *samādhi* are sure to follow. There's no need to do anything. Later, when one gets good at practice one doesn't need to aim any longer. One can just look at the target and shoot.

AC: In other words, mindfulness isn't the lead quality? Other qualities lead it?

SUP: When we practice *satipaṭṭhāna* meditation, only when *vīriya*, *vitakka* and *vicāra* are developed does *sati* arise. So *vīriya* or ardent energy, the application of effort, and *vitakka*, aiming or focusing must be there in order for *sati* to arise in practice. This is what happens when we practice *satipaṭṭhāna*.

This is not ordinary *vīriya*. This is called *ātāpa* – ardent energy which is not cool, not sluggish but always wakeful, alert, active. When I was young, I played marbles and when learning how to shoot I found that when there was too much effort, when I used too much energy, the marble would go off, go past the marble I wanted to hit. And when there was too little energy it wouldn't be effective either. So the effort had to be just right. This is what the quality of aiming does: it makes our quality of effort just right.

When there's ardent effort and application of aiming, then the marble connects with the marble you're trying to hit. There's *vicāra*, the quality of rubbing that occurs when it connects just right with the marble, and then joy arises, *pīti*. This is what happens in *satipaṭṭhāna* practice.

The *sati* that arises in practice behaves the way a stone does when dropped into water. When dropped in water, the stone sinks on the spot. The characteristic of *sati* is that it doesn't skim the surface of an object. It goes right into the object, like a stone dropped in water. Think of it like that.

The function of *sati* is to not lose sight of the object. It keeps the object in sight at all times. It also penetrates the object. *Sati* is non-superficiality. It does not allow the object go out of sight.

It brings the observing mind face to face with the arising object. When the mind is face to face with the object, then *kilesas* (greed, anger, and ignorance) have no opportunity to enter the mind. This is how *sati* manifests – as protecting the mind, guarding it from *kilesas*.

When *sati* is steadfast, the mind stays present, right there. It doesn't scatter. This is *samādhi,* when the mind is collected on the object. *Sati* brings *samādhi* with it. So when one applies ardent effort to observe the arising object again and again and again, along with the *jhānic* factor of aiming, then *sati* becomes steadfast and *samādhi* arises. When this happens, in fact, if you look at the amount of energy that is involved in one moment like that, it's nothing much, but if you have one moment of consciousness after another without a gap so that they are contiguous, one oc-curring right after the other, then amazing energy is generated. This is because this clean mind has the same nature, one fol-lowing another, the things are of the same nature, that's how the energy can be built. The mind with *viriya, vitakka, sati* and *samādhi* is pure and clean; this occurs again and again and again without a gap, so that they are contiguous.

AC: In other words, when *right effort* is made in this way, knowledge naturally follows?

SUP: The nature of energy is that when the clear mind occurs just once, it's not strong. But when that clear clean mind – which in itself is not strong – arises continuously, then auto-matically becomes very strong because each occurrence has the same nature and there is no gap between them.

Present at the same time is *vitakka* – the mind accurately placed on the object, and momentary concentration, the mind falling collectedly on the object. What happens is that when the mind observes the rising of the abdomen (when one inhales) and knows the qualities such as stiffness or tension – the mind sees true nature. And the same with the falling sensation of the abdomen (when one exhales) – one perceives movement and possibly other objects as well, and as such, one knows the true nature that is present at that moment. This is *paññā* (wisdom or insight knowledge). This is knowing correctly. And it's knowing completely and for oneself.

Here we are talking about *sampajañña* (clear comprehension). This knowing, the way one knows, is not confused, not mixed up; one thing and another are not mixed up. One sees clearly. There's stiffness and knowing of it. There's tension and knowing of it. So one sees the different phenomena as being distinct, not mixed up, one and the other.

This type of knowledge is far better than the type of knowledge gained from reading or from thinking about things. For this type of knowledge, the Buddha used the word *sampajañña*. We touched upon this earlier. The Buddha used the word *sampajāno* to mean 'one who knows in this way', one who 'clearly comprehends.' The noun, knowledge, is *sampajañña*. So when we study *satipatthana* we know this; and when we practice *satipatthana* we understand it.

The Buddha talked about how what we come to know in practice is like what we know when we eat food – when we chew the food we know what it tastes like and we know very clearly what that taste is. And the characteristics that make up what we could call true nature, *sabhāva*. They are also called *sarasa*, because they are like the flavors that we find in food. And when we practice, as when we eat food, we know the flavors for ourselves. This is knowing for oneself.

Mind and matter, *nāma* and *rūpa*, each have their own individual characteristics. One is not the same as the other. When we start to practice, this is the first thing we come to know, that mind is one thing and matter is another. When we continue to observe true nature, when we continue to practice and our knowledge of the true nature becomes mature, when we are able to see it more deeply, then we come to see what things have in common.

So we come to see that hearing, seeing, smelling, touching, tasting, hot, cold and so on, all these things appear and disappear, they arise and then pass away, and in arising and passing away, all the things we experience are the same. This is called *vipassana* knowledge. So whatever it is, if we want to know true nature, if we want to know how things truly are, we must observe what is there when it happens. We have to observe what happens when it happens. This is known as *anupassanā*, repeated observation.

Anupassanā is a word found in the *Satipatthāna Sutta*. It is something you have to work to develop. You have to practice to develop the skill to observe. The way the word *anupassī* is explained in the Commentary is that first one practices: tries again and again to develop the ability to observe with mindfulness. Second, by continually developing the ability, one gains the skill to dwell seeing, dwell observing with mindfulness. That observation is called *anupassanā*.

To re-cap, *anupassī* is explained in two ways: *anupassanā-sīlo*, developing the ability to observe, and *anupassamāno*, meaning one can just do it, one can keep on dwelling with mindfulness.

The process of coming to know true nature or developing this ability to observe with mindfulness is like looking at something from a distance and then coming closer and closer to it. Like a line of ants, when seen from a distance, appears to be a rope or stick – we mistake reality. We see something but we see it wrongly, as a rope or stick. And as we move closer and closer, finally we see it rightly as a procession of ants. Coming even closer, we see that each ant is moving in a different way.

First of all, you have to practice to develop this skill and then when you practice enough, you gain the skill. Practice makes perfect. This is what's involved in meditation. If you don't practice, without working to develop the skill, you're never going to know. Knowledge without practice is merely reflection. Practice brings experiential knowledge.

For example, someone puts a bowl of sugar in front of you and says "sugar is sweet." You see the sugar cubes and hear "sugar is sweet." That's one way of knowing that sugar is sweet. But when you take the sugar cube and place it on your tongue, you come to know the true nature of sugar as sweet. So how are these two different?

AC: One is direct experience of course, and one is imagination.

SUP: *Sūta-maya-ñāṇa* is what you read or hear, *cinta-maya-ñāṇa* is what you know by reflecting, and *bhāvanā-maya-ñāṇa* is knowledge born of meditation.

Take for example, while sitting there: when you clench your fist what do you find? There are three levels on which you can see: the form, the manner, and the true nature. The form: the shape of the hand. Manner or position is how it's clenched: in a fist. But these aren't true nature. At the start of practice, one's mind goes to the form or the manner, the way its clenched. These aren't true nature, but because the mind isn't going anywhere else it's still good. Later, when one continues to observe, one's mind becomes collected and one starts to know. When the mind is mindful of stiffness, it knows the stiffness. If the mind falls on tightness, one knows the tightness. One can also know the uncomfortable feeling. All these things are true nature.

At the start, we see things mixed up with either the manner or the form, but as we keep going we come to see just the *true nature*, only the true nature and nothing else. When your hand becomes hot, don't you want to open it again? That's because it's uncomfortable. Because there is the intention to open the hand, you release the hand. By releasing it ... opening it feels comfortable. And the fingers have to be released one by one. You have to move them slowly, very, very slowly, bit by bit, observing one moment after another. Slowly! Very slowly!

So how do you feel right now?

AC: I feel relieved, as I imagine everyone in this country will feel through the process of reconciliation, by mindfully opening their hearts and minds, and releasing the clenched fist of anger.

SUP: Looking for the *dhamma* you find it in yourself, that's all. You come to see how change takes place, the old being replaced by the new.

AC: Sayadaw-gyi, as a monk who has trained for many decades in the Buddhist scriptures as well as in practice, you have explained, combining theory and practice, how *sati* – mindfulness – develops. Mindfulness is everywhere today, and in some circles among those who guide others in mindfulness, they are somewhat proud that they are not teaching it through the lens of Buddhism. In fact, some feel they are doing a service to humanity to have removed the *Buddha, Dhamma* and *Sangha* – all those so called "cultural and religious trappings" from the essence, pure mindfulness. And in so doing, mindfulness is often taught as a tool for effectiveness, productivity, efficiency, mind-state management, and so on. I'm not saying this in a negative sense, but the argument goes: when mindfulness is so powerful on its own, why bring religion and culture into it?

SUP: Such work is not grounded. That means, it has no foundation. One has to start with the basics. The basics are to know the qualities of the *Buddha*, *Dhamma* and *Sangha*. After that, one should continue with morality and the duties of a human being, going hand in hand. These basics are missing.

AC: What about the argument that *sīla* – Right Speech and Right Action – refraining from stealing, slander and intoxicants and so on, are universal ethics and not owned by Buddhism? Why can't one practice mindfulness with basic ethical intelligence as the basis and still proceed wisely and confidently along the journey of life? Why does one have to be a Buddhist?

SUP: Inherently, the teaching of the Buddha is not a religion. Religion has faith as its base and is accomplished only through faith. If one wants to know the *dhamma* experientially, the best way is to practice.

"If one does good, one will get a good result. If one does bad, there will be a bad result." This is like understanding that when one eats nutritious food, one can digest it and gain strength; the knowledge that eating what is poisonous or unsuitable for one brings harm. This basic intelligence is needed. There are pure and clean actions, speech, and mentality, and unwholesome actions, speech, and mentality. Pure and clean actions, speech and thought bring good results. Unwholesome actions, speech and thought bring bad results. If one has that basic knowledge, one can meditate.

AC: That's basic *dhamma* intelligence?

SUP: That knowledge as a base is enough to be able to practice. The base is very important. When constructing a building, only if the foundation is firm will the building last long.

Some kinds of earth require one to place pilings to make a good foundation. If the fundamental practice is missing, it's not possible to go on to the higher practice.

AC: Is *sati* – mindfulness – always a wholesome state? Always? It's never wrong? Or are there instances when you can practice wrong mindfulness? In other words, we are familiar with the terms Right Speech and Wrong Speech; Right View and Wrong View; and so on. Then we come to Right *Sati*, or Right Mindfulness. Is there such a thing as Wrong *Sati?* Wrong mindfulness? Or is *sati* always Right?

SUP: More important than having *sati* is *yoniso manasikāra*. *Manasikāra* means aim or objective. Whatever one is doing, one should aim to make errors minimal and make things correct. Like when driving, steering correctly to get to our desired destination. One must follow the road. It's like that. More than *sati*, one's aim or objective is important.

AC: Will you please give an example of a wrong objective – steering in the right and the wrong way?

SUP: For example, if you go to a dangerous place, you should prepare whatever is needed to remain free of trouble. That sort of thing. So that danger doesn't occur, on your side, you need good protection. You make preparations so that you won't err. This is steering in the right way. You have to drive within your lane, according to the rules of the road. You can't straddle the line, driving in between the lanes.

AC: Allow me to ask the question another way: What if I were a president, a cabinet minister, the speaker of the house, an MP here in Myanmar, or even a general and I trained my military in mindfulness? I trained them to exercise mindfully, speaking and eating mindfully, and I even had them undergo mindful target training.

In addition, as King Bimbisara did, I had them believing that the enemy was out to kill us and that they wanted to disturb our peace and tranquility, harm our families and take our land. Worse yet, convert us to their religion. And as 'loyal soldiers, mindful soldiers,' we believed that we were defending our homeland, our peace and values. But it turned out to be a lie, a hoax. It was a manipulation by the top leaders to accumulate more wealth and power. Call this basic dictatorship. It may even be basic democracy in the Western world. Regardless, is that the wrong application of *sati?* Wrong mindfulness? Because the goal is wrong?

SUP: One's objective is important. There are two kinds of *sati*: *sammāsati* and *micchāsati*. *Sammāsati* (right *sati*) is involved in work that is pure and clean. *Micchāsati* is involved in *akusala*, unwholesome deeds. That is called *micchāsati* or wrong sati.

Sammāsati follows a clean objective. *Micchāsati* arises when one has an impure objective. When harming others or causing them pain, the awareness involved is not right sati. It is wrong mindfulness. One has to develop awareness in a blameless way.

AC: A final question for today, if I may: It seems that much of what you share – your *dhamma* advice – is about recognizing that 'we are all in this together', that no one lives in isolation, no one is an island. In other words, we need each other to survive, to learn from, and grow – children with parents, students with teachers, citizens and leaders, so many essential relationships to wisely consider. In the South African culture, they have the concept of *ubuntu* – which means, "I cannot be who I am without you."

Translator: We have it here in Burma too.

AC: How interesting. Because, the issue you speak of, that 'of exchanging ourselves for others,' seems to be closely linked or essentially the same as *ubuntu*. And if we could truly learn how to '*ubuntify*' ourselves, so to speak, the qualities of *mettā, karuṇā* and *muditāa,* along with most every other beautiful state of mind, would develop, naturally. And if we could merge foresight – our future-oriented compassionate open eyes – into *ubuntu,* we may well preserve life, survive as a species, and prevent a sixth extinction; maybe.

My question: Is there a Pali Buddhist word for this *ubuntification* of being? Again, the meaning of *ubuntu,* as I understand it, is that 'I am who I am because of you.' Or, 'I become human through my relationships.' In other words, 'no one can become free in a vacuum.' Is there a Pali word for this idea, for the idea of how we become free and human through each other?

SUP: There is a worldly saying, not a Pali one. It goes like this, "If he's not part of it, it can't be done. But he alone can't do it. If you aren't part of it, it can't be done, but you alone can't do it. Without me, it can't be done. But I alone can't do it. Only when he, you, and I are part of it can everything be done." This is a Burmese saying.

AC: Beautiful. This points to our inherent mutuality, our inter-relatedness with all things. Do you use this concept in your *dhamma* teachings? And does this concept have significance or have a corollary concept for a *Bodhisattva* (one who has made a vow to become a Buddha)? Because, as I understand it, a *Bodhisattva* cannot accomplish the development of *pāramī* without others. Is this essentially the same concept?

SUP: It is not possible to fulfill *pāramīs* by oneself, alone.

Pāramī can be fulfilled in a constructive way. Things to one's liking. And they can also be fulfilled in a destructive way, by having to endure something done against one. Either way, *pāramī* is fulfilled.

In the case of *Devadatta* (the Buddha's nemesis), in his previous lives he helped the Buddha to fulfill *pāramī* in a destructive way. But the Buddha-to-be endured all these destructive actions, knowing that it is only through encountering people who oppose one that the *pāramī* of *khanti*, or patient forbearance, can be accomplished. Because of his forbearance in the face of destructive actions, starting from his first life as a *Bodhisattva* up until his last existence when he became the Buddha, *Devas* and humans understood how great his patience was and revered him.

AC: It strikes me that this concept could have great importance within the development of SQ in leadership.

SUP: When there is a difference of viewpoints, SQ is important for people to be reunited. People who have good SQ are straightforward, they automatically go the right way.

AC: Would you illuminate the meaning of the word *pāramī* more fully? In addition, how can *pāramī* be embraced by leaders as the basis of *ubuntu* and compassion, and therefore, develop high-quality SQ-based leadership?

SUP: I rarely use the word *pāramī*, but in my *dhamma* teachings, my encouragement amounts to developing *pāramī*.

The word *pāramī* means, with a basic good mental attitude, doing things for others and at the same time making oneself great. Only a high-level person, an excellent person, can do that type of work. Therefore, the literal meaning of *pāramī* is that which makes a person excellent. It is how they become excellent.

When a person does not think of his or her own benefit but works for the benefit of others, how will people feel when they see this? They will feel that person is really good, truly superior – this idea arises in their minds. That is how the word *parama* arises. *Parama* in Pali means superior, excellent. What makes you

perceive that person as excellent, or *parama*, is *pāramī*, the cause
for that person to be perceived as excellent.

This word *pāramī* does not refer to the work done by people
who only think of themselves and lack *mettā* and *karuṇā*. Only
what is done with great *mettā* and *karuṇā* for the welfare and
benefit of others is true *pāramī*. That is why the word *pāramī* is
explained as 'the work of someone who is an excellent person.'
It is the cause for a person to be called 'good.' Or, it is what an
excellent person does. That is called *pāramī*.

When we speak about the *dhamma*, although we don't use the
word *pāramī*, we are talking about how excellent people behave,
what things they carry out: "If you follow this path, your status
in life becomes excellent." That's what we say. Although the
word *pāramī* is not used, it is the work of *pāramī*, every day.

Doing things solely for one's own benefit with no *mettā*, no
karuṇā is not *pāramī*. For example, if you give somebody something, you shouldn't have any expectations, such as, "He'll be
indebted to me, he'll love me, he'll be friendly to me." That is
not *pāramī*. Your personal benefit is involved. But when you give
something and think, "May this person be happy because they
have this thing to use," you are giving so that the other person
will be happy. Or thinking, "May what they lack be fulfilled."
One is working in order to solve the problem of not having
enough, to make the other person feel happy. This is *pāramī*.

When one puts one's own interest at the forefront and does
things to help others, that is not *pāramī*. When one puts others'
interest at the forefront, instead of self-interest, whatever one
does for the benefit of others is *pāramī*. People think that this
word *pāramī* means something very great.

And it is a great word. It means the work of excellent people.
This work in itself is great. It isn't the work of ordinary people.

AC: What is the relationship of practicing *satipaṭṭhāna* and the development of *pāramī*?

SUP: When you practice *satipaṭṭhāna*, *sīla* is involved, as well as *samādhi* and *paññā*. One's physical, verbal, and mental behavior all become purified. One doesn't make trouble for anybody else. Although one is doing this for oneself, because one doesn't cause trouble for anyone, it is *pāramī*.

Letting go of your own personal benefit and working for the benefit of others without expectation of return is *pāramī*. When one keeps *sīla* purely for the benefit of one's own liberation from the suffering of existence, when one practices to develop good *samādhi*, when one works to develop knowledge, when one practices *satipaṭṭhāna* meditation, this is *pāramī* for one's own benefit. One doesn't trouble anyone else, and one works for one's own benefit.

The word *pāramī* has two meanings: the cause for people to be excellent *(paramānaṃ bhāvo pāramī* in Pali) and the work of excellent people *(paramānaṃ kammaṃ pāramī)*. When one carries out work for others' benefit in an honest way, that causes others to see that person as excellent, superior, or *parama* in Pali. Therefore, it is said, *paramānaṃ bhāvo pāramī*. The work they are doing is the cause for the knowledge to arise in the viewer's mind that "this person is really excellent *(parama)*." Therefore, the work that they are doing is called *pāramī*. A person who is excellent like that will only do things that are blameless and pure. That blameless, pure work is the work of excellent people. That is why the word *pāramī* is also defined as *paramānaṃ kammaṃ* – the work of excellent people.

AC: Thank you Sir. And may the good leaders of your country and those in other countries as well, embrace the consciousness of *ubuntu* and the action of striving for excellence through *pāramī*.

IT'S IMPORTANT *to* BE
a TRUE HUMAN BEING

..

ALAN CLEMENTS: This will be the conclusion of our series of conversations titled, "Wisdom for the World and Dhamma Advice to My Nation" to also be published in the forthcoming book *Aung San Suu Kyi and Burma's Voices of Freedom.*

Tonight I would like to ask you for your *dhamma* advice to the people outside of Myanmar, those foreigners who will visit your country in the years to come, as well as all others worldwide with their eyes on Myanmar, watching the developments, with the birth of democracy, respect for human rights, and a vision of national reconciliation.

My question: What advice would you care to offer the good people who will either visit your country or those who are attentive, looking for ways to understand and possibly help the people of Myanmar? I might add, there are close to a million foreigners in Burma right now. The hotels are filled, often months in advance. Temples are packed with visitors. And millions more are on their way. I would not be surprised if your meditation center and Mahasi Yeitkha as well, become filled with eager foreigners wanting to practice *Satipaṭṭhāna* at the epicenter of where the worldwide mass lay-mindfulness movement began some 70 years ago. And each one of these visitors will bring a little piece of their own democracy here, their own unique experience of freedom.

It's an exciting time for Daw Aung San Kyi and the people of your country. It has been a 27-year long nonviolent 'revolution of the spirit,' and now the next phase of that revolution has begun; call it "the reconciliation revolution" through *mettā* and *karunā* or, in your language, "the SQ revolution."

What might you wish to share with these good people?

VENERABLE SAYADAW U PANDITA: It's natural for people to help each other, and this should be done without self-interest. One shouldn't want to get something out of it, and one should help with *mettā* and *karuṇā*. This is correct, to help in this way, to discard selfish interest and to help with loving kindness and compassion. When you give to another, whether it's giving to an individual or giving to a group, whether you give a material thing or whether you give advice or whatever it is that's needed, it should be done with the attitude, "may the person receiving this be happy to have it." One should not have an expectation of return for oneself. If one wants to profit from it for oneself, that's not truly helping. One must not boast to the world, "My country, my people, can help." Only when help is pure and true does it truly help. It should be help offered without *lobha*, without greed, without selfish interest.

Further, when you help people who are limited or lacking in some way, giving them what they need, fulfilling what is missing or lacking for them, then you should do so with the wish, "May they be well, may they be happy," and this attitude should permeate your mind so that the mind is fresh and moist with this feeling. Just as one should have this wish for the welfare of those one is helping – this attitude of pure *mettā* – so too, when one sees that people are lacking what they need, one should cultivate the attitude, "May they not suffer," and then go about trying to remove their suffering, relieving them from their struggle. The attitude of compassion, *karuṇā*, is very important.

When we give, when we help others while free of self-interest and with a basis of loving kindness and compassion, then we'll be happy with the results. One won't have envy for the recipients in seeing their good situation. One will be joyous to see their good situation. And because one has helped with an attitude of wanting their welfare, selflessly, then one doesn't feel jealous, one doesn't feel that they wish they hadn't given. The quality of happiness for another's good situation is *muditā*. This is based on *mettā* and *karuṇā*. Without a basis of true loving kindness and compassion, this *muditā* will not arise.

Further, both the giver and the receiver, although separated by different countries, should have the attitude they are related; one should have the attitude that one is helping one's relatives. Asia is one of the continents of the world and Asians are related to each other as relatives on the Asian continent. And the people of the world are all the same in being human. So we're related as world relatives.

People from other continents are related to each other although their continent is different; they're not related as continental relatives but as world relatives. And according to the Buddha, the people of the world have lived countless lifetimes before this one. We've all been related in one way or another, as father and son or brother and sister and so on. In countless ways we've been related to everyone. This is what is said in the texts and one should try to have this attitude.

In addition to this way of being – related on two or three levels – the Buddha taught so that people can become related by the way of *dhamma*, related by *dhamma* blood. The *dhamma* is that which bears the *dhamma* bearer, the one who knows the correct method and puts it into practice. It lifts one up so that one doesn't go down into the four lower realms of *Apāya* and so that one doesn't wander a long time in *saṃsāra*.

This *dhamma* is what the Buddha searched for and found. People who have faith in the *dhamma* – relatives – practice it, and through this practice are able to live happily in this very life as well as become free of existential suffering. People who reach this level of developing the *dhamma* blood within themselves become related by *dhamma* blood. Between them there is mutual understanding, trust and friendliness.

So, think about your own life, as you ask this question. Before the practice, how was it? And after practice, learning about the *dhamma*, how was it?

The Buddha taught the *dhamma* so that people who were related in worldly ways automatically would become related by *dhamma*. And those who practice and develop the *dhamma* blood don't make distinctions about nationality. They don't have this attitude that "I am this," or "I am this or that." We're all the same.

For us monks, whatever foreigner comes here to practice, if he or she practices the *dhamma* with respect and care, they become close, a *dhamma* relative. So think about that – when you practiced, did this type of feeling arise in you? Did you feel connected?

AC: Deeply, sir, like family.

SUP: People of the world are related in three worldly ways, but this is not enough to solve the complex problems that exist in society now. They will continue to exist. Only if people become related through *dhamma* blood will social problems gradually become weaker and weaker until finally people can gain peace.

AC: The people of your country have suffered, greatly. Equally, they have inspired many of us in the world to become more courageous in transforming our own sufferings and, more-over, putting ourselves in the mind and body of others, to feel and to act compassionately. What would you like to leave us as a final statement, to your people, and to everyone in the world?

SUP: If one is born a human, it's important to be a true human being, and it's important to have a humane mentality. And one should also search for a way to come to know what is true, to know the true *dhamma*, and to walk the path of *dhamma*. One should walk this straight path because if one walks it one will reach a safe destination. This is what's really important, these three things.

In this regard, in the time of the Buddha there was a *deva* (a celestial being) who came to see the Buddha, and he said that the beings of the world are tangled up in a tangle, both inside and outside; who is it that can untangle this tangle?

The Buddha's reply was very simple. With *sīla* or morality as a basis, if one works to develop *samādhi* and *paññā*, or concentration and wisdom, to completion then social problems will be resolved. That's the essence.

Many people lack basic morality and no longer fulfill their duties as humans in society. Without morality and not perform-ing their duties, their minds are no longer upright. Such people are crooked, and because of that social problems have arisen which are nearly impossible to solve. But if people learn to keep basic *sīla* and fulfill their human duties, when they start to get the benefits from this and they recognize these benefits, then they will follow this path, realizing it is good. They will follow this path honestly. They will no longer want to get the better of others. They won't want to make a profit at the expense of others.

When people keep morality, fulfill their human duties and understand the benefits, they become honest and upright. Then our existence in society becomes one of interdependence, like the Burmese saying, "The island depends on the grass and the grass depends on the island." When there is grass growing on the shore, the island can withstand the water striking it. When a wave comes in, what happens? It doesn't erode the shore. The grass protects the shore. And the shore holds the grasses so they can grow. If there were this kind of mutual preservation in society, the world would become fresh and peaceful again. This is called in Pali *aññoññanissita*, or 'each relying on the other' – interdependence. Without morality, without fulfilling social duties and without honesty, then interdependence or mutual preservation cannot occur. Only with these as a basis can these occur.

When people don't have basic morality and don't fulfill their duties or responsibilities in society, what happens between people? There is immorality and people's character is not upright. But if both self and others keep morality and fulfill their responsibilities, then their character is sure to become upright. If that thrives within society then there will be mindful interdependence. If that happens, the world will become a happy place.

AC: *Sādhu, sādhu, sādhu.* Thank you, from my heart.

SUP: Thank the Buddha, they are the Buddha's teachings.

AC: *Sādhu* to the Buddha. *Sādhu* to the Dhamma. *Sādhu* to the Sangha. *Sādhu* to you, Sir. *Sādhu* to Daw Aung San Suu Kyi and the National League for Democracy, and all the courageous people of your country too. *Sādhu* to the people who sacrificed their lives for this birth of freedom. *Sādhu* to everyone on having the moral courage to admit their mistakes, reconciling with each other, and bringing peace and harmony to your beloved Myanmar. And beyond, to the people around the world. May we all take greater risks to put ourselves into the shoes of each other, and the unborn, and to act compassionately, now and forever.

With good will for the entire cosmos,
cultivate a limitless heart:
Above, below, & all around,
unobstructed, without hostility or hate.

Sutta Nipāta 1.150

A Conversation with
VENERABLE SAYADAW U PANDITA, 1996
BY ALAN CLEMENTS

..

ALAN CLEMENTS: What is the basis of genuine dialogue, say, when two people or parties disagree with the others opinion and or position?

VENERABLE SAYADAW U PANDITA: Truth. The Buddha made this point clear. If truth is the basis of a discussion then there's possibility. Otherwise, one will tend to stay entangled in one's views biased by fear and ignorance.

AC: Who determines the truth?

SUP: Freedom is the best yardstick of determining anything of value.

AC: What is the essential difference in attitude of a Bodhisattva — a being striving for Buddhahood in order to help as many beings awaken as possible — and say, a *puthajjana* — one who, as theory states, is unenlightened but sincerely strives for full liberation — Arahantship? As you know, this fundamental distinction is the major difference in Mahayana and Theravada doctrine. Perhaps you could shed some light on the difference? Not many Asian Theravada teachers, if any, talk about this basic difference.

SUP: The difference is one of motivation. The motivation of a being striving for Buddhahood — a Bodhisatta — is more noble than someone who is striving just for their own liberation alone. Also, a Bodhisatta's dhamma zeal, or chanda, is much stronger. Another major difference is compassion. A Bodhisatta will be profoundly moved by compassion. Whereby the one aspiring for self-liberation is working only for his or her own attainment and realization. In other words, self-liberating types are primarily concerned with only passing the examination, while a Bodhisatta aspires to pass with distinction. Of course, by passing with distinctions you will be much more effective in helping others.

AC: I would like to pursue the issue from the angle of dhamma attitude, or right understanding. You clearly advocate and train others to pursue self-liberation. In so doing you exhort your students to restrain the senses and to see the dangers in pursuing sense pleasures. In addition, you work from a basic premise, in your words, "one must begin to see the inherent flaws of nāma-rūpa, that is — all mental and physical phenomena are subject to three common characteristics, that of anicca or impermanence, anatta or emptiness, and dukkha or suffering." Essentially, what I hear you saying is that the basic fabric of existence — consciousness itself — and every facet of conditioned experience upon that fabric — is fundamentally flawed due to the fact that it changes by nature, is empty of a permanent self, and therefore inherently unsatisfactory. Am I misrepresenting you?

SUP: Please continue.

AC: So, the spiritual seeker motivated by self-liberation must step out of life so to speak, remove him / herself from people, renounce relationships, at least while they are in retreat, and submit fully to the training of intensive meditation until they are enlightened, so the story goes. On the other hand, a Bodhisatta has an opposite attitude, he or she is not renouncing life. They are approaching the issue of liberation from a radically different motivation. Am I right in saying that the Bodhisatta is in need of people? That he or she wants to be near people, close to them and involved with them? Isn't the Bodhisatta saying, I want to make people my highest priority? In fact, I need to be with people because without others compassion is empty. It would be fantasy compassion. So, I need people, I need existence, to fulfill my aspiration as a Bodhisatta. My question is this. How to reconcile this attitudinal difference. On the one hand for a self-liberating type seeing the essential flaws in nāma-rūpa. And the Bodhisattva who needs people to accomplish the development of the *paramis*. Couldn't you turn the whole thing around and say that without the *kilesas* — afflictive mind states – and nāma-rūpa – the mind and body — I would never find liberation from them? In other words, I need life to know life. I need bondage to know release from it?

SUP: Let me say it this way. The Bodhisatta's attitude would be just like a parents' attitude towards their children. Profound parents have mettā and karuṇā for their children. Whatever situation they are in, whether delinquent, bad or good, the parents will always have mettā and karuṇā. They constantly strive for their childrens' happiness. They always want to be near them and not separated from them. Also, such parents are able to endure any response from their children. They are able to endure any form of suffering inflicted upon them by their children. No matter what it is, even if they are insulted, abused or criticized, profound parents maintain love and compassion towards their children. They keep it foremost in their heart towards their beloved children. So too will a Bodhisatta endure samsaric sufferings. He or she will endure any insult by beings, any abuse, any transgression. Because, for the true Bodhisattva, all beings are his children. They are his life. However, the inherent flaws of nāma-rūpa, of existence itself, remains the same. Reality is reality. In fact, seeing these flaws, that of anicca, anatta and dukkha, more distinctly gives rise to greater compassion in an individual. The distinction of the two types, the self-liberator and the Bodhisatta, is one of how you handle that discovery. One seeks to go the distance as fast and they can. And the Bodhisatta chooses to endure overwhelming samsaric sufferings for the sake of developing the paramis — the ten accomplishments of a Buddha — for the sake of optimizing his skill in helping others.

AC: Would you please say a more about the motivation of a Bodhisatta?

SUP: A Bodhisatta is ready to take pain and suffer loss, come what may, for the sake of realizing the goal of full awakening. A Bodhisatta is dedicated to harmlessness — not harming others. Mahakaruṇā, or great compassion, is the mark of a genuine Bodhisatta. Compassion is responsible for dhamma zeal — the staying power, or spiritual stamina, to face and endure any and all obstacles with courage. The Bodhisatta endeavors to withstand any samsaric sufferings — anything. Not just ordinary sufferings but everything. And you can use your imagination here to try to fathom this point. Look around you. Look at the sufferings people must endure. A Bodhisatta welcomes it. A Bodhisatta thrives on it. Lives for it. Why? For a Bodhisatta compassion must be the foremost quality in everything he or she does. Consider the Bodhisatta as a 'Great Mother' who endures everything for the sake of her child's welfare. The Bodhisatta follows in the spirit of 'Great Motherhood' by including more and more people in their sphere of love and compassion. One's heart must become big. But compassion is not enough in supporting the welfare of others. Unless one knows what should be abstained from and what should be observed there will be misguidance. One must have wisdom or pañña. Without wisdom you cannot differentiate between abstention and observance. Compassion alone will not serve the purpose. There must be pañña when associating with people. Understand it in this way, one associates with karuṇā and one disassociates with pañña. Both qualities are essential when supporting the welfare of others.

AC: In what way do you use the word 'disassociate' with pañña?

SUP: Compassion brings you intimately close to people. Pañña allows you to understand what to do and how to succeed in the task of helping others overcome their suffering. As you work with others, you work with yourself in developing the paramis. You must have these dual qualities. If you only feel compassion you don't know what's right or wrong, skillful or unskillful, or what to abstain from and what to observe. Without wisdom you'll be misguided, and you will misguide others as well. In other words, you will not know what should or should not be done. Only with pañña can one truly work for the welfare of others. Compassion is not enough.

Let me put it another way, only when one fulfills the causes will one accomplish the effects. Accomplishment of causes leads to the fulfillment of results. But first there must be self-fulfillment, then fulfillment for others. Without fulfilling the causes, and one is claiming results, such a person is an opportunist. If one has fulfilled the causes and results, and is not helping others, then, that would be selfish. After the Bodhisatta fulfilled the causes, such as the full development of the pāramīs and the complete eradication of the kilesas, the result was Buddhahood. Only then did he work for the welfare of others. It seems that you've taken a liking to Mahayana Buddhism?

AC: Was the Buddha born in Burma? (Sayadaw-gyi's laughter) I'm trying to understand the nature of compassion, that's all. And if that requires inquiring within other traditions, well, why not? I'm also very much engaged in the world today and that has brought my dhamma life front and center into a quest to understand interrelatedness, or how to find liberation through living.

SUP: Many years ago I met a Mahayana Buddhist monk in Hawaii who asked me about the issue of self-liberation versus working for the liberation of others. I asked him, "if you're both stuck in the mud how can you save each other?" After some dialogue, the monk agreed that one of the two "stuck monks" must have a sure foot on solid ground before he could help the other. Helping oneself and helping others are both important aspects of the dhamma. Thus the Buddha stated, liberating oneself is most important. After that one can help to liberate others. Not the other way around.

AC: Isn't that a bit idealistic? Don't they both go hand-in-hand, as one seeks liberation so too we help others? Of course, within our means.

SUP: You mean to say that you do them at the same time?

AC: Yes. That's been my experience.

SUP: Would you give an example of how that works?

AC: You just used the example of two people stuck in mud. If I may, I'd like to see that they both made it out of the mud, jumped into the ocean to wash the mud off, but in so doing, they got in over their heads. How I see how both aspects of the dhamma go hand-in-hand is like this: perhaps the stronger of the two, the one with more physical strength or perhaps the wiser of the two, sees the shore and decides that they must get back to solid ground. This person assists the other. He swims with him on his back, and while doing so, perhaps encourages the other fellow not to lose faith, or not to give up. If the stronger one tires, perhaps he shows the weaker one how to float for a moment and maybe, just maybe he regains his strength. If not, he grabs him and keep swimming towards the shore. Fundamentally, what I'm saying is that I'm not working from the basis of perfection or even an ideal. In fact, perfection has been a type of unseen noose around my neck. Always striving for an impossible goal and therefore always graded by a lie: my unwillingness to be human and as such, true to my own instincts. Which, in this case, means, helping others as I help myself.

SUP: But first you must know how to swim. You must have proficiency. If both are not skilled it won't help. Please explain how you see it will help? If they are in shallow water it may help, but in deep water it won't.

AC: Obviously I don't understand the magnitude or depth of samsaric waters. Nevertheless, the hand-in-hand method of living the dharma seems closer to my truth.

SUP: One must be proficient first. You must first train in life-saving before you can help another. Your point is not realistic.

AC: I'll give another example. Everyone with functioning legs can generally walk. Now, two people are on a trek together, but they miscalculated their food and water needs. Soon their supplies run out and they are not skilled in knowing which plants to eat nor can they locate water. But they are determined to strive on with the hopes of reaching the next village. One of the two falls ill. The stronger of the two assists and perhaps carries the other along as best he can. Isn't this a realistic possibility?

SUP: It is, but you must have the strength to put him on your back.

AC: Yes, but my point is, even if he dies along the way you do what you can to help your friend. Even if you both die, you both died with honor and courage and dignity. Thus, hand-in-hand, or assisting others as we assist ourselves, makes the most sense to me.

SUP: Yes, but you must be stronger than others. You must first build up your strength. Otherwise, you would be deluded to go on such a trek.

AC: I'm not saying that you save anyone, but you do the best you can considering the circumstances. But it may be that you both make it out alive.

SUP: Of course, that's realistic. But this is not a superior ability to save others. You're talking 'only' about a very ordinary ability.

AC: Would you give an example of a superior quality of saving others?

SUP: For example, in the story of the hermit Sumedha. At that time he could have become an Arahant, he had the qualities during Dipankara Buddha's time. But he renounced an opportunity to become an Arahant because of seeing the danger in samsara. Beings driven by fear and craving going round and round in a mad swirl of suffering. Sumedha had great compassion well-up in him. And with this great karuṇā he had the notion, "an able man like myself should not just swim across from this bank to the other shore alone. I should assist others by becoming a Buddha." On that he renounced his opportunity to become an Arahant in order to strive for Buddhahood. This is not ordinary. This is a super-normal quality. Because of this we have the dhamma today. This is the sāsana of Buddha Gotama, who was Sumedha at that time.

AC: I have another question about reversing dhamma attitude; seeing value in adversaries. Maybe Sayadaw could help me with this. We all know the story of Devadatta — the Buddha's cousin. At the time of Devadatta's death some monks celebrated, but the Buddha demanded of them to stop, saying that Devadatta would become a Pacceka Buddha[7] in a future existence. I have also read, the exact place I'm not sure, perhaps in the Jatakas, Sayadaw can correct me if wrong, where the Buddha explained that without Devadatta having shadowed him for innumerable existences — harassing him, tormenting him, aggressively seeking his demise and even his death — he would never have been able to mature khanti pāramitā, or patience. I find this very interesting. In saying this, wasn't the Buddha praising Devadatta, not so much as a person, but as an epic opportunity — an archetypal manifestation of an adversarial energy — and without Devadatta's aggression — his role as the Bodhisatta's nemesis, well, Buddhahood would have been impossible? The interface of opposites served the ultimate spiritual purpose, equally, for both individuals. In other words, the confluence of opposing energies

---

7 A 'silent Buddha,' one who is fully enlightened but cannot teach how to become enlightened.

became the nexus for dhamma transformation. Patience and compassion developed from wise engagement with disagreeable situations. Was the Buddha referring to conventional obstacles as dhamma opportunities?

SUP: Yes, in a destructive way Devadatta was helping the Bodhisattva. Like the opposition party in Parliament criticizing the government in a destructive way. If skillfully dealt with, adversaries assist governments by forcing them to rethink their position and possibly refine their party's policies.

AC: But is it ever possible to be certain, say, in the case of Devadatta, that his actions were ultimately wrong? After all they were leading him to his own Buddhahood. My concern here is this: why draw distinctions, ever? Why should life be a wrong condition to be made right? Why not be beyond doing, choosing, seeking, but equally, do, choose and seek, if you know what I mean?

SUP: Causes have effects, simple! It wasn't that Devadatta in every existence was doing unwholesome deeds. Take his final moments of life. At the last minute prior to his death, he confessed openly to the Buddha. He realized his wrong doings, his shortcomings and with honesty in his heart he offered his body, skin and bones, openly to the Buddha. He was remorseful. He knew the Buddha was right and he was wrong. His last minute kusalas were noble...quite praiseworthy.

AC: Let me say it more directly. Correct me if I'm wrong, but from a strictly Theravadan point of view, birth and the life that follows, is essentially a nightmare, a bad dream. Samsara is dukkha, no matter how you cut it, full stop. And who could argue the point, really? With life, so many bad things can happen: torture, rape, starvation, genocide, extinction. It can be a horror show. So, what I'm hearing is that proper dhamma

attitude, the profound type of intention that really seeks freedom, is essentially a quality of striving for nirvana, extinguish
the defilements, and get the heck out of Life. Am I wrong?

SUP: The Buddha taught suffering and a release from it.
But continue.

AC: My question is this; is there any place in your understanding from either a personal application of dhamma or from
the study of the Pali Canon, that lust, desire, anger, torment,
indeed any of the afflictive emotions, from mild to obsessive
forms, even madness itself, rather than seeing them as evil or
demonic and therefore destructive, can they be viewed in an
opposite way, that is to say, constructively — in service of liberation and freedom? Call it a non-pathological spiritual alchemy
if you will. In other words, please talk to me about turning hell
into heaven or poison into wine — the transformation of negative energies into positive forces. This issue interests me a great
deal at this point in my life. It's plain easy to love loving people
and downright difficult to be patient with aggressive or even
judgmental people. And how much more difficult it would be
to compassionately embrace a man who raped my partner, or a
group of generals who ethnically cleansed areas of my country.
I watched this when I was in the former-Yugoslavia during the
final year of their conflict. It was pure madness.

SUP: Interesting question. There is an explanation of this
found in Paṭṭhāna — the book on Conditional Relations within
the Abhidhamma — of how akusala, or unwholesome mind
states, can be a cause or condition for kusala or wholesome states
of mind. However, three main conditions must first be met. To
begin, you need a kalyāṇa mitta or a skillful spiritual friend,
and then with proper dhamma consideration, afflictive mind
states can be an object of meditation. That is, if one applies satī

or mindfulness. Without right causes there will be no dhamma results.

AC: What is 'proper dhamma consideration' in this case?

SUP: A person should consider in this way: an unwholesome state of mind has come upon me, and if I allow this akusala condition to persist I'll drown in this akusala. This negativity will engulf my being. It will shroud my consciousness negatively, so I should befriend this condition and skillfully use it to my benefit. Thus, this agonizing condition will be used to my benefit and eventually for the benefit of others. It's essential that one knows this state as it really is — the first Noble Truth of Buddha's enlightenment, that of Dukkha Sacca, the Truth of Suffering. You fully hold to this knowledge, and only this: 'this is the Truth of Suffering.' From there the akusala becomes one's sole object of attention. He or she is mindful of it, meditates on it, knowing the truth as truth, knowing things as they exist, here and now, and only now. The pure and basic truth I'm experiencing akusala, that's all, just as it is, now. This is called vipassanā kusala or impeccable mindfulness at the moment of occurrence. This is cultivating insight knowledge. So, in this way, an akusala condition serves as a cause for kusala.

AC: Could you give a practical example of this, say from the texts?

SUP: At one time there was an elder monk named Mahavisa who was quite learned in scriptures. He reflected one day on the limitations of mere scriptural knowledge. Thus, he aspired to become an Arahant. Not only Arahantship, but he wanted to eradicate all the kilesas in a very short period of time. In fact, just a few days time. He was quite ambitious. So, he went into a forest for solitude, determined to attain liberation by Visuddhi Parinna, the confession day of the monks. He wanted to pronounce his freedom to everyone on that day. However, he wasn't so fortunate. He not only failed to attain his goal of Arahantship but was unable to realize any stage of freedom. Even worse, all the other monks were able to achieve Arahantship on the day he desired. Thus, everyone celebrated except poor Mahavisa. He was miserable and for the next nineteen years Mahavisa felt grief and sadness. But those nineteen years were not wasted. They served to strengthen his resolve to become fully enlightened. Why? Because he vigilantly continued his dhamma practice, reflecting with courage in the way mentioned earlier. He was no ordinary monk. He was brave. See, this elder's domanassa or grief was the type of dosa or anger that sinks inward. It was a self-directed sadness. This kind of anger is not the type that often arises when someone insults you whereby you react. Rather, it arose from self-reflection. It arose from knowing that he was unable to free himself. Therefore, he felt a self-directed sadness. In this way, his misery, grief and sadness became conditions for him to turn into a beneficial purpose. They became the support for him to perform wholesome mind states in the face of unwholesome ones. So, in this way akusala mind states support the arousal of kusala. Akusala generates kusala when right conditions are involved. Without proper conditions there are no dhamma results. In this way, one sees that everything is not only interrelated in a lawful way, it can be an opportunity for liberation.

Take for example snake venom. It cannot be used as anti-venom without first being mixed and processed further. Some additives must be there in order for it to save lives. So too can akusalas, these so-called inner poisons, can be made into good use by mixing them with satīpaṭṭhāna — intelligent awareness. But if akusalas are not processed with satīpaṭṭhāna they become more and more poisonous. In this way poison becomes a condition for purity.

AC: Moving along to another subject, please. Throughout my 17 years of association with you I cannot recall hearing you give a dhamma talk about the subject of 'nonduality,' at least never with the use of that word. I'd like to keep the question quite simple to start. Is there a Buddhist Pali word for nonduality?

SUP: (With a smile) How do you spell it?

AC: N...o...n...d...u...a...l...i...t...y. (Sayadaw picks up his English to Pali dictionary, thumbs through it, then closes it).

SUP: (Shaking his head) No such word. (Pausing for a long time) Do you mean the view that there's no right or wrong, sort of what you were alluding to earlier, when you said, "beyond doing, choosing, seeking, but equally, to do, choose and seek?"

AC: Sure, let's start there. Why make any distinctions at all?

SUP: We say, in seeing just seeing, in hearing just hearing, present and pure presence of mind. In this way, yes, there's the suspension of this or that. Just a moment of reality, as it really is. This is called an indeterminate state of consciousness, neither akusala nor kusala. This is suññata, suchness, voidness of self. Call it zero.

AC: Are anatta and suññata the same or different?

SUP: Identical, one and the same, just different usage.

AC: So the undifferentiated state of mind I'm referring to means 'embodying zero' as a way of being. Only now, unbound, containing all things, all time, past, present and future. My question is this: how to go from two, to one, to zero?

SUP: Are you asking about the 'view of nondoing?'

AC: Let's start there?

SUP: This is called akiriyavāda, or the doctrine of nondoing. Is it that you don't like doing?

AC: Why differentiate doing from nondoing?

SUP: So you like being swept downstream thinking it's up stream?

AC: Why consider it up or down. In an infinite circumstance there's no absolute direction, no centrality, no ultimate vantage point. The ocean is boundless. It Is.

SUP: The ocean is also deep. Are you over your head?

AC: It doesn't feel that way.

SUP: It may be time to swim (both of us laughing). Look at it this way. With clear considerations you speak and act with good results. With unwise consideration you get the opposite. This "It Is" is conditioned. It is interdependent. It is a cause and effect interrelated eternity. You know that. And the layers of this truth are deep and subtle. Now because someone might assume they are comfortably floating on the surface of the ocean, doesn't mean they will either remain floating or even float in a favorable direction. It might appear that way for a while, maybe a long while, a few days or years or even a decade or two, maybe longer but it's a rudderless existence. Anusaya kilesas do not simply disappear by floating on top of them. Samsaric currents are strong and powerful and beings cannot escape those currents by floating to the other shore. Throw anything at all in the ocean and see where it goes. This is why we direct the yogis to observe their minds — to note seeing as merely seeing, and hearing as hearing, nothing more. Not to go beyond that. Otherwise it will be kusala or akusala. In this way one withdraws themselves from the cycle of becoming on deeper and more subtle levels. But at first you draw distinctions to lead yourself out of the current of delusion, out of the habitual responses to avoid or attach to this or that sense perception.

We've come into being as humans. There is nothing we can do about that, except not to perpetuate the cycle of kusala and akusala. Since we've come into existence, we note this effect. This effect is with us all the time. The value or result of awareness is that it eradicates the cause of becoming. So, we note the existing things which are present — seeing, hearing, and so on. When there's no cause, there will be no effect, no becoming and no suffering. By observing effects, we eradicate causes. Therefore, no effects. Without effects there's no becoming. Humans are like fruit trees and as such, we try not to let it grow into a new tree. This is basic Theravada: the end of suffering is the end of becoming.

AC: This leads me to the next question. Theravada is often criticized as essentially an escapist doctrine and practice. How would you respond to that?

SUP: You know as well as I do that there will be all kinds of views about everything. Theravada Buddhism is not exempt. Some will call it as you said, escapist. While others will have the compassion and zeal to give the method of escaping to others. Just as someone who is trained in medicine, they will have proficiency in medicine and healing. Some might just use their knowledge on themselves, for their own benefit. Others might go beyond that and teach others in medicine. Why? They appreciate good health and know the pain of illness and disease. From compassion a person desires to help others and with wisdom they give the remedy. Compassion seeks to help others escape suffering. Wisdom knows the way to do this. When you are sick and in distress do you not desire to escape the affliction? Wouldn't you do anything to get better?

AC: Yes. Unless it was terminal, then I think, I'd just hang out, keep on living my dream until I died.

SUP: Would you be an escapist for desiring to get rid of your pain?

AC: No. Seems practical and wise.

SUP: Theravada practice is of three kinds — dāna, sīla and bhāvanā. They are the cure for kilesa agony. They are not about selfishness. There are two types of enemies, internal and external. The internal enemies are more dangerous and only when one gains victory over the internal enemies will one be able to control the faculties. When we can control or safeguard ourselves, we can then consider the welfare of others. Greed and anger are dangerous qualities. You watch the news. It's a dangerous world. And these dangers root in consciousness. If we can't control these destructive fires, we not only harm ourselves but we are dangerous to others as well. Only when we subdue and eradicate the internal afflictions do we uplift ourselves, uplift our dignity and our honor. From this we not only become true human beings we become noble human beings. So, by eradicating inner enemies we indirectly safeguard others by not harming others. If we are free of the kilesas we safeguard others. In this way two things are accomplished together. So, the truly cultured human is one who doesn't harm others, knowingly or unknowingly. And this is accomplished by the dual qualities of paññā and karuṇā, which we discussed before. With wisdom one safeguards oneself and others, and with compassion we safeguard others, and likewise we're not defiling ourselves. This is so simple to understand. You drive a car. Of course, when you're driving it's important to avoid accidents. If you follow the rules and stay aware, vigilantly aware, others will not be harmed by you. You're not dangerous. This is respectful and beneficial to others. Is this escaping?

AC: No. It's practical, respectful, and necessary.

SUP: This is the Theravada doctrine. Not to harm others because of your mistakes. Of course, you may be harmed by other's mistakes but do not seek to harm others through your mistakes. Buddhism teaches us not to be a nuisance.

AC: Reducing fear in the world by subduing projection and blame?

SUP: Stop at red lights. Don't cross lanes haphazardly, so on and so forth. Most of all stay awake, be aware and be present. That's all.

AC: Is it possible to discuss in any realistic way the consciousness of a liberated being — an Arahant — without being fully liberated oneself?

SUP: No, not directly, but you can through deduction and inference.

AC: Well then, I'll ask a question. I've come to understand through your dhamma talks and reading dhamma literature that in the mind of an Arahant the kilesas are eradicated. What does 'eradicated' mean?

SUP: It means the anusaya kilesas, the latent or dormant unwholesome tendencies within consciousness are cut off, completely. Gone. Even if there are conditions for kilesas to arise they don't and can't.

AC: For clarification sake, kilesas mean any form of defilement within consciousness — energies rooted in greed, anger or delusion?

SUP: That's right.

AC: So, what you're saying is that under no circumstance whatsoever can greed, anger or delusion arise in the consciousness of a fully liberated being?

SUP: That's right. Such mind states as you described cease to exist. However, certain propensities or tendencies or personality traits still exist. These vāsanas, as we call them in Pali, remain intact. Say for example, there was an individual who before attaining this stage of full liberation, or Arahantship, was proud or conceited and had the habit of denigrating or belittling others. These vāsanas or psychological habits would remain with him, but the kilesas would be eradicated. The difference is the intention or cetanā. A fully awakened being would not have aversion as a cetanā, but he or she could still denigrate others so to speak.

AC: Can you give an example of how vasana and kilesa are different?

SUP: Vāsanas are like the smell of whisky or the scent of honey that remains in a bottle once it has been emptied and washed. Kilesas are the substance, vāsanas are the smell. But vāsanas are not found in the mind of Buddhas. There is no tendency from the past that exists in the mind of a Buddha.

AC: Can you tell from observation whether someone is fully liberated?

SUP: There is one story found in the traditional Buddhist literature that speaks of one follower of an Arahant. The student attended on his teacher in many ways. He once asked the Arahant what were the characteristics of a fully enlightened being? The Arahant replied that even though you may follow an Arahant day and night, observing carefully his speech and demeanor, you would never come to know through ordinary eyes if he was indeed an Arahant or not. He went onto to say, but one test to determine Arahantship is through fear. If at any time fear arises this person is not an Arahant. An Arahant is free of fear. Fear arises from anger or dosa, and anger roots in moha or ignorance. So, fear is a good test of one's freedom.

Another test is whether raga, or lust or passion arises. By lust I mean lust for a man towards a woman or woman towards a man — sexual passion for another person. An Arahant is free of raga. The only practical way to at least get a feel of the Arahant's mind is to practice vipassana up to the stage of sankharupekkha nana or the stage of equanimity towards all mental and physical formations. At that stage of insight one can get a taste of the Arahant's mind.

AC: I'd like to end by asking your advice about an important issue. The other day when we were walking through the monastery you turned and said, "you were the one responsible for first bringing me to the west." You then asked if I thought Theravada had really taken root in America? In all honesty, I said, I wasn't sure. Something is taking root but I'm not sure it could be called Theravada. You then asked me, "what was it?" I replied, "I think it's fair to say that everyone who teaches does so as best as they can from their personal experience." Which brings me to the question. What advice would you give to western dhamma teachers and to those who may come to them for guidance as they continue in their own ways to spread the Dharma in the west?

SUP: The most important thing is to know the true qualities of a spiritual friend — a kalyāna mitta. Eloquence, humor or intensity of speech isn't what I mean. Those are only superficial qualities. The main quality of a kalyāna mitta is his or her depth — the twin qualities of wisdom and compassion. They should be well developed. Next, one must approach this spiritual friend and practice dhamma. Only after you practice and achieve good results then you can take that method as beneficial and correct. A teacher's personality can be like honey but unless it's free and not sticky the fly will die. So the method of freedom should exceed attraction to personalities.

Another aspect of a strong spiritual teacher is that they do not criticize others. Anyone who understands the true dhamma, especially after they have reached the stage of Ariya, there will be no such thing as uplifting oneself or denigrating others. The Buddha made it clear that the objective of dhamma was to end dukkha, to extinguish the internal fires of, greed, hatred and ignorance. In so doing the goal of practice may be the same yet the approach may be different.

For example, all know there are many different schools of medicine. The point is to know medicine, to help others, be of great value to others. But first one needs training. They approach a good school with competent teachers. Through persistence and great dedication, one gets a preliminary degree in both theory and a bit of practice. Then if one wants to specialize, become highly proficient, one goes on or goes further in their training. Nevertheless, no matter how well trained someone becomes, medicine is a complex area of study and as the saying goes, nothing can fully prepare you for the test of application once you are outside of school. But without training you're a quack and a danger to society. You're dealing with people in life and death circumstances and you better know what you're doing. However, as I said, when one goes outside into the real practice of medicine one may encounter certain diseases never before known or come across. So instead of treating them in the usual way, or the traditional way, the doctor may invent a personal approach to the treatment of that disease. But in so doing, a doctor may treat just the symptoms and the symptoms may subside in the patient. The patient may temporarily even feel good again and the doctor may shout success. This isn't the dhamma. This is nothing more than smothering a fire with a blanket, thus forcing the fire to go underground where it resurfaces someplace else at a later time. All the while it smolders in the soil of their spirit.

Kilesas are a complex issue and treating them is equally complex. So, when a doctor treats a patient with his or her own method, providing it actual works, such a person may take pride in that cure and might denigrate others. In fact, this is common. How do you say? It often comes with the territory. But there really is no need for pride or conceit. Arrogance is a rather lame response. Nevertheless, it is quite common. Sometimes the arrogant rooster gets his head cut off before the hens. So one must be watchful of 'roostering' so to speak.

On the other hand, there are teachers who are quite intelligent but cunning. This is a type of fear. These teachers, and we have them in Burma, often like their popularity as dhamma teachers more than the dhamma itself. Of course, they would never admit to this, but we see it even in Burma. It's quite common. Since the wind blows in many directions and since some teachers may be like a flag, in other words, they enjoy being at the top of the pole, so they behave like a good flag, and flap in the right direction. But sadly, they are controlled by the wind. The wind is the need for popularity and they're controlled by it. But because they're presently the flag — and often a mere symbol for their followers — tied up high at the top of the pole, they do their duty as a good flag does and just keep blowing in the direction of the wind. This is spineless. Flags take no stand. Rather flags are attached to poles, not the other way around. A pole might stand but flags come and go and no matter what, with so much wind flapping, the flag eventually becomes tattered and ripped. People like this wear out in time. It's natural.

A true spiritual friend isn't concerned with being a symbol for people. They're courageous, fearless and willing to stand alone if need be. The dhamma needs no support, it's free.

A final example and we'll end. Say, you want to pay your respects to the Shwedagon Pagoda in Yangon. Now there are four main gates in which you can approach the pagoda. So, one person goes up from one particular gate, another person goes up yet another gate and so on. Isn't it silly to criticize others for going up another gate other than the one you went up? Really, this is unnecessary and foolish. What's important is to see and to visit the pagoda, to be inspired by its splendor, and not how you come to the pagoda. That's missing the point. But now the times have changed, we have elevators at the Shwedagon, so it's much easier for you to get to the top. You can't say that it is wrong or incorrect. The purpose is the main criteria. To reach the pagoda, pay your respects and carry that inspiration with you when you leave is what is important. Nevertheless, if you take the wrong way up you will end up in the wrong place. Now, one who teaches the wrong way to the pagoda must indeed be criticized. Not in a negative sense but with encouragement and with love in the heart. This is the correct type of criticism. It brings unity of purpose.

AC: Thank you Sir. Thank you very much.

Left to right: *U Khin Hlaing* (translator) *Venerable Sayadaw U Pandita* and *Alan Clements* in Sayadaw's cottage where the interviews took place.

Alan Clements and his colleague *Dr Jeannine Davies* during the interview sessions with *Venerable Sayadaw U Pandita* in Burma February 2016.

The Venerable Sayadaw U Pandita of Burma

Alan Clements and his friend *Derek Kaye* (who filmed the interview sessions) with *Venerable Sayadaw U Pandita* in Burma, February 2016.

Venerable Sayadaw U Pandita

Venerable Sayadaw U Pandita was both a Buddhist scholar
and meditation master.

Daw Aung San Suu Kyi paying her respects to *Venerable Sayadaw U Pandita* seated at his desk Nov 15, 2010, 2 days after being released from house arrest.

Venerable Sayadaw U Pandita during an interview session with a yogi (meditator).

Alan Clements at his ordination in 1979; one of the first Westerners to ordain as a monk in Burma and practice mindfulness meditation under both *Mahasi Sayadaw* and his successor *Sayadaw U Pantita*.

Venerable Mahasi Sayadaw as a young monk about to enter his first insight meditation retreat in the 1940s.

မဟာစည်ဆရာတော်ကြီးနှင့် ဆရာတော်

U Pandita with *Mahasi Sayadaw* soon after arriving to *Mahasi Sasana Yeiktha* in the mid-1950s

Sayadaw U Pandita as a young monk in his early 20s.

Shwe Oo Min Sayadaw and *Sayadaw U Pandita* as young monks, and life long friends.

Venerable Sayadaw U Pandita at his Yangon monastery, Panditarma, passed away on April 16, 2016,

Saya U Tin Oo, former General of the Army and NLD co-founder, paying his final resepcts to his teacher.

Resident Nuns gather around the body of their teacher, *Sayadaw U Pandita*, at his Yangon monastery, Panditarma.

A gathering of devotees paying their final respects to their teacher, *Venenerable Sayadaw U Pandita*.

The *Venerable Sayadaw U Pandita's* cremation on April 22, 2016 in Burma.

Sayadawgyi's remains, life's destiny for all Beings.

Venerable Sayadaw U Pandita a few years before he
passed away at 95 years old.

AUTHORS

..

ALAN CLEMENTS

Boston born Alan Clements, after leaving the University of Virginia in his second year, went to the East and become one of the first Westerners to ordain as a Buddhist monk in Myanmar (formerly known as Burma), where he lived at the Mahasi Sasana Yeiktha (MSY) Mindfulness Meditation Centre Yangon (formerly Rangoon) for nearly four years, training in both the practice and teaching of Satipatthana Vipassana (insight) meditation and Buddhist psychology (Abhidhamma), under the guidance of his preceptor the Venerable Mahasi Sayadaw, and his successor Sayadaw U Pandita.

In 1984, forced to leave the monastery by Burma's military authorities, with no reason given, Clements returned to the West and through invitation, lectured widely on the "wisdom of mindfulness," in addition to leading numerous mindfulness-based meditation retreats and trainings throughout the US, Australia, and Canada, including assisting a three month mindfulness teacher training with Sayadaw U Pandita, at the Insight Meditation Society (IMS), in Massachusetts.

In 1988, Alan integrated into his classical Buddhist training a social and political awareness that included global human rights, environmental sanity, and the preciousness of everyday freedom. His efforts working on behalf of oppressed peoples led a former director of Amnesty International to call Alan "one of the most important and compelling voices of our times."

As an investigative journalist Alan has lived in some of the most highly volatile areas of the world. In the jungles of Burma, in 1990, he was one of the first eye-witnesses to document the mass oppression of ethnic minorities by Burma's military dictatorship, which resulted in his first book, *"Burma: The Next Killing Fields?"* (with a foreword by the Dalai Lama).

Shortly thereafter, Alan was invited to the former-Yugoslavia by a senior officer for the United Nations, where, based in Zagreb during the final year of the war, wrote the film *"Burning"* while consulting with NGO's and the United Nation's on the "vital role of consciousness in understanding human rights, freedom, and peace."

In 1995, a French publisher asked Alan to attempt reentering Burma for the purpose of meeting Aung San Suu Kyi, the leader of her country's pro-democracy movement and the recipient of 1991's Nobel Peace Prize. Just released after six years of incarceration, Alan invited Aung San Suu Kyi to share her story with the world, for the purpose of illuminating the philosophical and spiritual underpinnings of her country's courageous nonviolent struggle for freedom, known as a "revolution of the spirit."

The transcripts of their six months of conversations were smuggled out of the country and became the book *"The Voice of Hope."* Translated into numerous languages, *The Voice of Hope* offers insight into the nature totalitarianism, freedom and non-violent revolution. Said the London Observer: "Clements is the perfect interlocutor....whatever the future of Burma, a possible future for politics itself is illuminated by these conversations."

Clements is also the co-author with Leslie Kean and a contributing photographer to *"Burma's Revolution of the Spirit"* (Aperture, NY) - a large format photographic tribute to Burma's nonviolent struggle for democracy, with a foreword by the Dalai Lama and essays by eight Nobel Peace laureates.

In addition, Clements was the script revisionist and principle adviser for *Beyond Rangoon* (Castle Rock Entertainment), a feature film depicting Burma's struggle for freedom, directed by John Boorman.

In 1999, Alan founded *World Dharma,* a nonsectarian, multicultural, trans-traditional organization of self-styled seekers, artists, writers, scholars, journalists, and activists dedicated to a trans-religious, trans-spiritual independent approach to personal and planetary transformation through the integration of radical authenticity, global human rights, mindful intelligence, and the experiential study of consciousness, with one's life expression through the arts, activism, and service.

In 2002 Alan wrote *"Instinct for Freedom—Finding Liberation Through Living"* (World Dharma Publications). As a spiritual/political memoir it chronicles his life-long pursuit of truth and freedom, while illuminating the framework of the World Dharma vision that forms the basis of the World Dharma Online Institute (WDOI) that he co-founded with his colleague, Jeannine Davies Ph.D., Vice-President of the Buddha Sasana Foundation.

Instinct for Freedom was nominated for the best spiritual teaching/ memoir by the National Spiritual Booksellers Association in 2003 and has been translated into a numerous languages.

Alan's most recent book, "*A Future to Believe In—108 Reflections on the Art and Activism of Freedom*" (World Dharma Publications, 2012), inspired by and dedicated to his daughter Bella, has received distinguished praise from numerous leaders and activists, including Dr. Helen Caldicott, Dr. Joanna Macy, Dr. Vandana Shiva, Bill McKibben, Paul Hawkin, and Derrick Jensen (the environmental poet laureate) who wrote:

"This culture is killing the planet. If we are to have any future at all, we must unlearn everything the culture has taught us and begin to listen to the planet, to listen to life — the core intelligence of nature and the human heart. This book not only helps us with the unlearning process — the greatest challenge humankind has ever faced — it provides the essential wisdom, the spiritual intelligence, to open ourselves to finally start to hear."

Alan is also a political and spiritual satirist, and performs his one person show "Spiritually Incorrect: In Defense of Being, Human," to audiences around the world, as benefits to raise awareness of global human rights, Burma's ongoing struggle for democracy, as well as to highlight the plight of prisoners of conscience, worldwide.

Clements has been interviewed on ABC's Nightline, CBS Evening News, Talk to America, CBC Canada, ABC National Australia, VOA, BBC, and by the New York Times, London Times, Time and Newsweek magazines, Yoga Journal, Conscious Living, Utne, and scores of other media worldwide.

In addition, Alan has presented to such organizations as Mikhail Gorbachev's State of The World Forum, The Soros Foundation, United Nations Association of San Francisco, the universities of California, Toronto, Sydney, and many others, including a keynote address at the John Ford Theater in Los Angeles for Amnesty International's 30th year anniversary.

www.AlanClements.com

..

"How to describe Alan's presentations? A tall order. Love poems/riffs/odes/chants to the goddesses of compassion, deeply inscribed with the blood of Burmese slaves, soldiers in Iraq, Palestinian children, freedom fighters anywhere. A momentary entry into an internal tête-à-tête, ad infinitum; a glimpse at all that inner discursive dialog which marks us unequivocally as members of the human race. Just in case we get too spiritual, let's not forget that we are required to, by nature, include everything. To paraphrase the Vietnamese monk Thich Nhat Hahn's poem, "Please Call Me by My True Names," I am both the 12-year-old raped girl and the pirate who raped her. It is difficult to reconcile seeming opposites, and it takes the heart of a poet. Thich Nhat Hahn is a poet; Alan is one as well."

MARCIA JACOBS, *a psychotherapist specializing in victims of war, rape, and trauma; a senior U.N. representative for refugees in Bosnia and Croatia, 1993–1997; and a former officer of the International War Crimes Tribunal*

"Alan's life is material for a legend. An intellectual artist, freedom fighter, former Buddhist monk, he shares his insights and experience with a passion rarely seen and even more rarely lived. He'll make you think and feel in ways that challenge your entire way of being."

CATHERINE INGRAM, *In the Footsteps of Gandhi and Passionate Presence*

"I have known Alan for close to three decades. He is my first call when I seek insight and candor concerning personal and professional advice. As a speaker, his eloquence moves audiences to ask the questions behind questions about how we live, why we work, and how it fits together. Alan's presence—his remarkable ability to engage an audience, connect with their heart—stands alongside the best talent I have ever seen."

ROBERT CHARTOFF, *Producer of Rocky, The Right Stuff, and Raging Bull.*

"One of the most important and compelling voices of our times... Alan Clements is a riveting communicator—challenging and inspiring. He articulates the essentials of courage and leadership in a way that can stir people from all sectors of society into action; his voice is not only a great contribution during these changeful times, it is a needed one."

JACK HEALY, *former director of Amnesty International, founder, Human Rights Action Center*

..

FERGUS HARLOW

Fergus Harlow is Alan Clements' assistant and co-author of the forthcoming four-volume book, *Burma's Voices of Freedom*. He "met" Alan first through Robert Anton Wilson's Maybe Logic Academy in 2004 and then on through the World Dharma Online Institute in 2007. Since early 2013, he has worked closely with Alan in all areas related to producing this and coming media projects. A keen student of the dharma, previous to this work he had been living and volunteering at various spiritual and retreat centres in the UK.